Mystery Mastery: Creating a Believable Mystery Novel

Michael F. Havelin

Mystery Mastery:
Creating a Believable Mystery Novel

Copyright 2014 by Michael F. Havelin
All rights reserved.

Written, designed and published by
Michael F. Havelin
Asheville, NC

ISBN-13: 978-0-9853553-4-0
ISBN-10: 0985355344

Paperback

Front Matter

Acknowledgements

Grace Lehto, friend and LocSec, for her editing insights and suggestions.

The WNCMysterians, my mystery writers' critique group in Asheville, North Carolina, for their insightful assistance. Check us out at http://www.wncmysterians.org.

The many qualified authors whose work I enjoyed and the tyros whose work I've suffered through. You've all taught me much.

Dedication

To anyone who has ever thought to or tried to, or even succeeded at writing a mystery, suspense, or adventure story. May we all become better writers through my efforts.

Disclosure

This is a book for the rank beginner with no writing experience, for the hopeful with an almost completed novel in a drawer somewhere, or for the published author. Hopefully, you have some skill with language usage and grammar and some experience with writing. Consider this book a supplement to all the other excellent books on mystery writing that you have read in the past or have in your reference library.

Mystery Mastery discusses basics such as character development, plot, setting, red herrings and the like, as it should, but there's more. There's also an extensive discussion of crimes and law relating to crime. It's important to know about the subject matter you're dealing with, and since we're writing about crime, we've got to know what the law thinks about it. Maybe you have additional insights from your own personal experience.

Let me remind you that all of this is my own opinions, developed over years as a reader and writer. I am not a *New York Times* best selling author, nor do I have a degree in literature or creative writing from a prominent university. I'm merely one more struggling writer with a few good ideas and no relatives in big time publishing or the movie business. I've worked as a photographer, an article writer, a book editor, and I published two national magazines for a number of years. I've studied law and have court experience, both as an attorney and as an interpreter, and I understand the legal concepts that give us our stories. I know how to structure a story, do thorough research, and move my characters from their initial situation all the way to the resolution of their various dilemmas.

As of this writing, I run a mystery writers critique group in Asheville, North Carolina, that's been going since 2009 (WNCMysterians.org). The insights from our group discussions and the hammering we do to beat one another's work into its best shape have been uniquely instructive. I'd like to pass on what I've learned there, as well as what I've learned through my own professional life.

I'd wish you luck at this point if I believed that's what it takes to succeed. But writing isn't luck. It's damn hard work. It requires commitment and long-term dedication to a project that might never see the light of day. It's a test of character, but not the fictional characters you create in your make-believe world. It's a test of your character.

Sowatchugonnado, eh?

How to Use This Book

This book is a broad guide to writing in general and writing mysteries in particular. It has some facts, plenty of opinions, and lots of suggestions.

Some sections can be considered reference material; others can be considered nonsense, and still others as sound advice. Make your own evaluations.

Weigh what I have to say, but remember that whatever is in this book is only one man's jaundice. If you find some useful information herein, that's great. But read more on how to write mysteries. Talk to other authors, lots of other authors. Gather advice from as many sources as you can. Toss out the ridiculous, sort through the rest for the best nuggets, then make your own decisions about your goals and the methods you'll use to realize them. No one person has all the answers for everyone else. If they say they do, they're sociopathic salesmen, charlatans, or perhaps politicians. In the end, whatever works for you is going to be the best method for you to use.

Experiment. Live your own life.

Table of Contents

Front Matter 3
    Acknowledgements 3
    Dedication 3
    Disclosure 4
    How to Use This Book 6

Opening Salvo 12
    Waiting for Your Muse 12
    Writer's Block 13
    The Rules 15
    Writer as Reader 16

Front-End Considerations 19
    Preparation 19
    Early decisions 19
    Who? 19
    What? 19
    Where? 20
    When? 20
    Why? 21
    Short Story or Novel? 22
    Series and/or Stand-alone? 23
    Research - Get your facts right! 24
        Exercises - Research 27
    Your Writing Place & Time 28
    The Coleridge Moment 29
    Self-discipline 30

    Mysterious Genres 32
    Cozy 33
    Noir 34
    Legal Thriller 35
        Exercises – Legal Thriller 36
    Police Procedural 37
        Exercises – Police 39

    Private Investigator – Hard-nosed or Otherwise 40
        Exercises – PI 41
    Amateur Crime Solver 42
        Exercises – Amateur Crime Solver 43

Preferred Crimes - Best & Worst 44

  Crimes Against Persons 47
    Homicide 47
        Exercises – Homicide 49
    Robbery 50
    Assault and Battery 52
        Exercises – Assault and/or Battery 53
    Human Trafficking - Kidnapping, Slavery, Illegal Immigration 54

  Crimes Against Property 55
    Conversion (Theft) 55
    Burglary 56
        Exercises – Robbery & Burglary 57
    Blackmail & Extortion 57
    Drug Crimes 58
    Arson 60
    Money Laundering 61

Sex Crimes 63
    Prostitution 63

Criminal Miscellany 66
Criminal Motives 66
    Profit (Greed) 67
    Power 69
    Revenge 71
    Love 72
    Misc. Motives 73

Manner, Cause & Mechanism of Death 75
    Autopsy 75
    Manner of Death 75

Cause of Death 76
Mechanism of Death 76
Weapons 77
Types of Weapons 78
Exercises – Personal Criminal Experiences 78
Writing Your Mystery 80
Words as tools 80
Sources of ideas 82
Characters 85
General suggestions 85
Sources for Characters 88
Clashing Opposites 89
Character Description 90
Exercises – Character Description 92
Protagonist 93
Exercises – Character 94
Sidekicks 96
Exercises – Sidekicks 97
Villains 98
Exercises – Villain 99
Henchmen 100
Exercises – Henchman (Henchpersons!) 101
Love Interest 102
Exercises – Love Interest 103
Cops 104
Exercises – Police 105
Minor Characters for Color 106
Point of View (POV) 107
General Considerations 107
First Person 108
Third Person - Omniscient Narrator or God Mode
.... 109
Exercises – POV 110

Plotting and Scheming 111
    Thinking Inside Out 111
    The Dreaded Outline... 113
    Outlining for Analysis 115
    Exercises – Analysis 116
    Who Done It?.. 117
    The Opening Situation 118
    The Hook 119
        Exercises – The Hook 120
    Foreshadowing 121
    Internal Continuity.. 122

Story Structure, Logic, & Time 124
    The Story Arc 124
    A Variety of Choices 125
    Linear Mode 126
    Flashback Mode 126
    Flash-forward Mode.. 126
    Reverse Mode... 127
    The Chapter 127
    The Scene 128
    Moving the Story Forward 128
    Pacing 129

Dialogue 131
    Let the Characters Speak for Themselves.......... 131
    Setting... 132
        Exercises – Setting 135

The Sensory Environment 137
    Exercises – Sensory Environment 138

Clues and Anti-clues 139
    Be Honest With Your Readers 139
    How Red Should a Herring Be? 141
    Self-discipline.. 142

After the Writing 144

The Problem: Getting It Right **144**
    Vocalizing - A Simple Technique That Works .. 146
Second (third, fourth, fifth, etc.) time around... 148
    Critique Groups 148
    Professional Editors 150
    The Axe as a Writing Tool 151
Technical Issues **152**
    Grammar & Spelling 152
    Vocabulary & Word Choice 153
Publishing **154**
    A Changed World 154
    The Traditional route 154
    Self-publishing 155
    The Electronic World 156
    Selling books 157
Appendices **158**
    Recommended Reading – Mystery Authors..... 158
    Recommended Reading – Reference 161
    Useful Websites **163**
    Critique Group Procedures **164**
Index **167**
About the Author **175**

Opening Salvo

Waiting for Your Muse

  If you postpone your writing in a wait for the notoriously recalcitrant Euterpe, the Muse of music and lyric poetry (or choose your own personal Muse), you'll still be waiting when the Grim Reaper comes to collect you. She isn't coming. That's her way, and you'd better understand that from the start.

  As for inspiration, there's no such thing. There are ideas that seem to spontaneously spring forth, like the title that you've worried about for two weeks, or the nugget that propels you into six months of sweaty work on the next novel. But ask any professional journalist, reporter or writer. A "real" writer should be able to sit down anywhere at any time and crank out however many words are needed. Are you a writer? Prove it.

  How do you prove it? By sitting yourself

down at the computer, typewriter, with a yellow pad and pencil, chisel and stone tablet, or whatever you prefer, and putting down words, thousands of words. You might have a problem getting started. The refrigerator might be calling you. The lawn may want mowing and the gutters may need cleaning. Ignore them. Ignore your friends, your spouse (spice?), your children, your job, that pending law suit. Once you start writing, you'll find a groove and the words will start to flow, faster and faster, until you reach your 80,000 word goal. Then you'll turn around and find that your Muse has been watching your progress over your shoulder. You see, it's you that has to inspire her, not the other way around. Tricky, huh? You'd better believe it. It took me years of artistic suffering to figure this out.

Writer's Block

I don't believe in writer's block.

I believe that plots can suddenly turn on you and leave you with temporarily unsolved dilemmas. I believe that there are times when your characters find themselves in a jam and can't find a way out for a while. I believe that the mind sometimes requires fallow periods in which to work at a subconscious level.

If you're at a "blocked" point and can't figure out what's happening, think about the problem before going to bed. In the "hypnagogic state," the half-awake moments before being fully awake the next morning, the answer may come to you from your subconscious mind. Let the magic of the subconscious help you out. Trust me. This works.

But writer's block? Sorry. There's no such thing in my world. There's laziness. There's the big football game that we have to watch. There might even be your kid's broken arm or the emergency birthing of your sole heir to interrupt your creative tsunami. But writer's block? To me, that's merely an excuse for not writing, and as such, it's not valid.

Mystery writing, any serious writing, is no mystery at all. Writing is a craft. Tools like grammar, punctuation and vocabulary can be learned and honed to respectable levels. But it requires commitment and focus on the job at hand.

Let's substitute the concept of "self discipline" for "writer's block." There are times when you simply have to force yourself into isolation from the mundane concerns of daily life and face the blank page. This requires personal courage. This is when the writer's true character shines through. This is when you find out whether you can do it, or if it's merely a fantasy and you should become a plumber's apprentice.

So sit yourself down and start writing.

The Rules

Rules? What rules? You mean there are really rules about how to write mysteries? I must be kidding.

W. Somerset Maugham is quoted as saying, "There are three rules for writing a novel. Unfortunately, no one knows what they are."

Actually, there are people who think there are rules, rules with a capital "R" that must be piously followed to create an interesting story and a saleable product. Piffle!

Writing rules are guidelines, and that's all. They are suggestions, perhaps echoes of works that have been successful in the past. But I encourage you, the writer, experienced or inexperienced, published or unpublished, well-connected or not, to find your own inner writer. Write what your story demands of you. If you can learn to pay attention to it, the story will tell you the truth, every time. Let your critics analyze your completed work and deduce "the rules" that you followed in writing it. What they have to say will be a revelation to you. You will have never thought of those things before.

You may come to the end of this book and decide that you haven't learned anything, that I haven't given you any solid advice on how to write a saleable piece of anything. Sorry if you feel that way. If that's the case, maybe you'd better go back to the bookstore (sic) and find that elusive copy of *Ten Ironclad Writing Rules That Will Teach You How to Write a New York Times Best Seller in Three Weeks or Less*. Memorize "The Rules" and let me know how your writing is going.

My responsibility here is not to give you inviolate rules for writing. Why is that? Isn't that why you bought this book? No. Simply stated, there aren't any rules. Every writer, on every individual project, must make a unique and personal journey. Every step is an experiment. Not only that, but what works for one story or book will not necessarily work for the next. Such an approach leads to formulaic writing, and you all know how boring that becomes in both the writing and in the reading.

I can give you what I surmise from my own life and writing experience, but I can't take the journey for you. It's yours alone, and must be taken alone. All I can do is point the way in the most general sense. Be courageous and take the first step. It will lead you to the next step, and the next, and the next. The journey will end some day with a completed project that is yours and yours alone.

Writer as Reader

To be a writer, you must be a reader. You must be familiar with the written word. And you must understand the genre you are taking on. This is done by immersing yourself in that sort of writing and analyzing the work of other authors.

Lawrence Block wrote about this in his helpful book *Writing the Novel from Plot to Print*. He goes into great detail about outlining the work of other authors to understand their handling of subject matter and seeing how they organize chapters and story flow. Though written in 1979, his advice is still pertinent and well taken. The principles remain the same.

My own advice is to saturate yourself in the written word generally, to read anything and everything you can lay your hands on. If your world is to be the world of words, go live there as soon as possible, and stay there for life.

Just as I've always been a writer, so I have also been a reader. I've been called a book worm as an insult, but I took it as a badge of recognition and a compliment. It showed me that I was on the right track toward the life I wanted, particularly when my self-confidence was ebbing due to rejection notices from magazine publishers and agents.

Let's talk about motivation a bit. Why do you want to write? Is it for the money? Good luck. There are many more starving writers than best selling authors. What about fame? Same thing. There's only so much room at the top of any pyramid, and to my cynical view, it goes to the well-connected or momentarily topical authors, or to already famous politicians or notorious serial murderers. For us mere mortals, it's a slog. If you want to be famous, kill a dozen innocent people and then write a memoir about your lousy upbringing by drunk and abusive parents and all the foster homes you've been in. You'll have the fame, but most states don't allow criminals to profit financially from their crimes.

How about the satisfaction of having written, of having completed a complex project? I feel that myself, usually with a degree of postpartum depression after having birthed the thing over those long, lonely months. But being a writer by nature (and perhaps nurture), I'm soon off into the next project and the depression lifts to reveal a new and exciting horizon filled with interesting characters and events.

Front-End Considerations

Preparation

Early decisions

You'll have to decide a few things right at the very start. Want a list? Okay. Use the venerable article writer's key, the vaunted five W's of journalism to settle the basics. You must decide the who, what, where, when, and why of your story.

Who?

Who is the story about? Who are your characters going to be? What relationships between them trigger the action and drive your story? What they do with and to one another is the meat of your work. Characters will be discussed in more detail later.

What?

What's the story about? Murder? Mayhem? Kidnapping? Terrorism? The ubiquitous profit motive? Pedophilia or sexual slavery? Look deep into the recesses of your twisted little mind. What's the worst you can come up with? What fascinates you but you would never actually dare to do? This is your opportunity.

Where?

Where is the story going to occur? Is it a tale of domestic murder at home in the basement or international intrigue in Europe's capitals? Will it happen in corporate offices in a major city or in the Canadian wilderness? It's your choice. You're the writer. You might even get to take that long wished for trip to an exotic locale for on-site research. Research expenses are tax deductible, so why not?

Setting is important to any good story. It might even be considered as another character. More on setting is coming later.

When?

When is the story going to happen? Is it set in a historical context, or a contemporary environment? Maybe it's going to happen in the future. Anything goes here. It's your story, and you can make it anything you want. Of course, the when question complicates your writing process.

If the story happened in the past, it's going to require factual research on how things and places were back then, how the politics and mechanical contrivances of the past actually worked.

If the story is contemporary, there's less of a problem if you've lived in the culture all your life. But be sure to get your facts right. Remember that there's a nit-picking reader out there in the bushes waiting to pounce on your smallest factual error.

If the story happens in the future, you have the problem of inventing a future world and its technology. Good luck with that. It's a monumental task to invent it all and have it make internal sense.

But it can be done.

Why?

Perhaps the most important early decision is the why of your tale. Why is it happening at all? What are the elements that set everything in motion, that cause the characters to act the way they do, to chase the goal or one another, to seek justice, vengeance, profit, or world dominance? What propels the story?

This isn't something to take lightly. The story has to be believable enough for a reader to plunk down their money, to enter your world, to suspend their disbelief, and to stay with your characters through to the end of the quest.

Short Story or Novel?

Well, it depends. Abraham Lincoln was once asked by a heckler, "Mr. Lincoln, how long do you think a man's legs should be?" Lincoln replied, "Long enough to reach the ground."

By analogy, the same is true for a story; it should be long enough to take a reader from the beginning all the way to the end. There's no set length for a short story, novella, or novel. There are guidelines that suggest ranges of page length or word count, but unless you have a publisher's contract in your hot little hand that specifies the finished length, it's up to you, or rather, it's up to the story. Keep writing until you reach the end, then stop.

For those of you who are rules oriented, here's a table of suggested lengths for different forms. It's compiled from a variety of sources. Some people might have other ideas. Do some research of your own.

Form	Typical Length
Flash Fiction	100 - 1,000 words
Short Story	2,000 - 7,500 words
Novellette	7,500 - 20,000 words
Novella	18,000 - 45,000 words
Novel	70,000 - 90,000 words
Epics	Over 110,000 words
Stage Play	90 to 120 pages
Movie Script	110 to 250 pages

My base suggestion is for you to tell your story in the most comfortable way and let the story decide how long it needs to be. If you plan to write 60,000 words, but the story writes to conclusion at 53,000, so be it.

When you reach the end, do go back and enrich your tale by adding more detail and description during the rewrite. But don't pad merely for the sake of word count. You'll ruin your tight writing.

If your story tends to run long, just be sure it isn't fluff that's doing the running. Each word in a manuscript should have a reason for being there. If there's no reason for it, get rid of it. Your writing will be better for the brutal editing.

Series and/or Stand-alone?

Is your story going to be a one-off tale? Are your characters going to flare into life for one adventure and then vanish into the mists of literary history forever?

Or are they going to appear again in further adventures, adventures that not only give them a career, but give you as the author a career as well? Think of the great series characters you've encountered in your reading life. Arthur Conan Doyle's Sherlock Holmes and Dr. Watson, Edgar

Rice Burroughs' Tarzan or John Carter, Agatha Christie's Miss Marple, Sue Grafton's Kinsey Millhone, Sara Paretsky's V.I. Warshawski, Michael Connolly's Lincoln Lawyer. How many others can you name?

To my mind, even a character designed for series work has to have adventures that can be read as stand-alone stories. Each adventure should be developed as an independent entity. The series' consistency, the thing that keeps your fans coming back to you, might be the characters, but the stories must vary in dilemmas, goals, and solutions in order to maintain your fans' interest over time. Don't forget; you are in competition with other authors and their characters.

Research - Get your facts right!

In anything you write, fact or fiction, you'd better have your facts correct. One mistake can cost you a fan or two or dozens. A hero or heroine's firearm error, for example, can make you look like a jerk and lose your credibility with readers in a heartbeat. Readers these days are much more sophisticated than in previous years. They know their locales, their weapons, their poisons, their forensics, and their legal processes. You'd better know all that and more yourself.

I love the Internet. It's made my research life so much easier. Sitting at my desk with a sandwich and a drink at hand, I can go online and get a basic understanding of anything I can think of. I can check grammatical usage and punctuation, find the preferred spelling of rarely used words, and see pictures of most things or activities. I can even buy research samples of many items I write about, such as old Spanish coins, simulated skeleton parts, firearms replicas, copies of old maps or other documents. What could be better?

I still go to libraries. In fact, I'm at the public library most days for one reason or another. But if I really want to isolate, it's now possible for me to stay home and do all I need to do to become a rich and famous author without having to deal with another human being at all.

You can learn what you want to learn at home. But although you can gather your facts, you might not gain the insight needed to put things together into a sensible and realistic amalgam. You still need to talk to an expert, maybe even handle the expert's samples, or have the expert show you how things fit together and actually work. The Internet can lead you to an expert, but a trip out into the world to meet the expert in person can't be beat.

It's been said that you're never more than a few steps removed from the expert you need to talk with. I've found this in my own work. Someone you know has a cousin who knows someone whose aunt is the forensic expert for the county. Bet on it. Make a couple of calls and see how it works. This "six degrees of separation" principle is so well-known that it's become the basis of a popular parlor game, *Six Degrees of Kevin Bacon*. Check it out in Wikipedia.

Some years ago I was working on an article about rattlesnakes. I had a rattler skin and several rattlesnake belt buckles to photograph, but what I needed was a photograph of a rattler's skull in biting position. Where was I going to find that? As it turned out, it was only two steps away.

I went to a local pet shop that handled exotic pets. A single question to the owner was answered with the phone number of a local reptile expert. I called him, learned he had the skull I needed, and that afternoon made a half hour visit to shoot my photograph. Voila!

Not only can you find what you want fairly easily, but most subject matter experts are more than willing to share their knowledge with you if you're working on a legitimate project. This help is usually given freely, with no thought of payment. If the expert demands payment, go find another, perhaps his colleague or competitor. There's always another source around somewhere.

When writing *The Assassin's Dilemma*, I wanted a location where a simple nonviolent guy would be able to commit suicide easily for the opening scene. I used to live in Rochester, New York where the Genesee River runs through the center of town, dropping over a series of serious waterfalls before flowing into Lake Ontario. I'd lived there so many years ago that my memory was indistinct. I went online and googled a map of downtown Rochester.

There was the river, and there were the two sets of waterfalls I remembered. Looking at close-up map views, I found the Pont de Rennes foot bridge. Some further research via a few more mouse clicks and I had my opening location nailed down. The pedestrian bridge had been the Platt Street Bridge when I was living there, but it had been revitalized as the city tried to put on a new face. It was the perfect locale for a suicide attempt.

Further along in the story, I needed a street scene in an industrial area. Google came to the rescue again, but this time, after figuring out where I wanted to place my action, I used the little orange figure in Google's street views to look the area over in detail. From their imaging, I could name the streets, see the buildings along them, and even describe the buildings and the varying views in different directions. For once, my location research didn't require an extended road trip that would take me away from home and regular work, cost me gas, meals, and hotel accommodation in a far off city. Thanks, Google.

Exercises - Research

- Use *Google Maps* to find the house where you grew up or spent part of your childhood. Use *Google Maps Street View*. Drag the little orange homunculus onto the map to look at your house and the surrounding environment.
- Find some other places you lived and take a look around. Read the street signs. See what changes have taken place.
- Pick a town randomly in a state other than your own and go there via Google. Look around. Find the city hall, several restaurants, industrial and residential areas. Enjoy the tour and come away with a basic knowledge of the town.
- Select a firearm your character is planning to use. Go find one. (Hint: call local gun or hunting clubs, sporting goods stores, pawn shops, your brother-in-law.) Handle the weapon. If possible, go to a range and fire it. How does it feel in your hand? How does it make you feel emotionally? Your story will be better for the experience and analysis.

Your Writing Place & Time

Writing is an isolating activity. It demands concentration and privacy. If you have a family, that's a problem. Get rid of them. Or . . . set a time when you are allowed to work without interruption and be sure that everyone understands that it's your specific and regular writing time. Nothing short of nuclear war should intervene.

By the way, don't quit your day job yet. Wait until your writing income is equal to or greater than the paycheck you've been bringing home from your fast food job. Writing might pay off in cash eventually, but at the beginning it only pays in smug self-satisfaction alternating with bouts of frustration and despair.

In any event, you need an inviolate place to write, whether it's the kitchen table before breakfast, or a dedicated spot in a corner of the basement or attic. The best arrangement is a flat surface where you can leave your work out and be sure it won't be disturbed by your spouse, your children, or the family cat.

These days, you need to have a computer with Internet access and a handy shelf for your reference materials. I use the Internet for much of my writing research, but I still have a physical library of books on writing techniques, a worn copy of *Roget's Thesaurus*, an unabridged dictionary, and numerous volumes with historical, geographic, forensic, medical, and firearms facts. Maybe I'm just old-fashioned, but I like the feel of a physical book.

Define the best writing environment you can for yourself. Be careful about providing yourself with a refrigerator though. You might end up more massive than the tome you set out to create. These days, exercise machines aren't too expensive. Find one at a garage sale for when you're having trouble thinking clearly. It might even save your life, if not your sanity.

The Coleridge Moment

Samuel Taylor Coleridge, the famous 16th century poet and opium smoker is reported to have awakened from an opium dream in 1797 with the entire 200-300 line text of *Kubla Khan* in his mind. He sat down to write it out, but was interrupted by someone at his door before he could get it all down on paper. An hour later, he returned to the task, but the moment was lost; except for scraps and vague impressions, the poem had vanished from his mind. The poem remains incomplete to this day. Author's note: It is still considered one of his three best poems.

For myself, I prefer (if not actually need) quiet and uninterrupted time in which to work. It's simply too easy to break my train of thought, to lose the thread of a scintillating paragraph, to garble the magical language that would win me a Golden Literati Award. Once gone, it's gone forever. Somehow the words never line up again in the exact same way. Don't let this happen to you.

Self-discipline

Above all else, you must get into the regular habit of writing every day.

In music, it's said that if you don't practice for one day, you'll notice it; if you don't practice for two days, your teacher will notice; but if you don't practice for three days, everyone notices.

You can draw a parallel analogy in writing. If you don't write for one day, you will know it and your guilt will start growing. If you don't write for two days, your Muse will notice and might go looking for someone else to bother. If you don't write for three days, you will lose your momentum and perhaps even say, "I'll get back to it tomorrow." And that can kill a project.

You have to keep the juices flowing. It's all right to sit down and crank out a few paragraphs, or even pages, of garbage. The book isn't done until it's done. Since you're in control, you can always throw out yesterday's junk and attack it again. But you have to keep at it.

Robert Heinlein developed six famous rules

for writers. I won't quote them all here. You can look them up yourself (that's called research). But I will cite the first two, which are: 1) write, and 2) finish what you write. Without those two maxims continuously running through your brain, all is lost, and you'd better go back to your day job at the donut shop.

    The problem with self-discipline is that you have to be your own strict taskmaster. No one will be sitting in your cell with you cracking a whip over your head and making an occasional agonizing stripe across your back. It comes down to self-flagellation for sure, and you have to accept that the time and effort expended is worth the pain.

    No product? Too bad. You'll never be a writer.

    Piles of paper covered with words? Now we're talking. No matter how bad it is, it's work product and it can be fixed. It still might not be worth it, but you'll at least have your self respect. And if you can find a skilled editor who believes in your story, you might have a best seller, or at least a saleable book.

    But whatever else you do, don't give up. Write regularly. Daily, if possible.

Mysterious Genres

What sort of a mystery are you going to write? The standard advice to new writers is "write what you know." But I think that's more true for style than for subject matter. You can always get the facts on any topic by doing a bit of research, but you have to at least enjoy the genre or the writing will be a slog instead of a stimulating activity.

If you love reading adventure stories that occur in exotic jungle locations, maybe that's what you should try to write. If you love the back alleys and bars of noir fiction, try that. If you're writing about a place and time you can't relate to in a genre that you can't stand, I hope your contract with that big publisher is paying you lots for your discomfort.

Cozy

Think Agatha Christie. Think Miss Marple. Think Merry Olde England, upper class criminals with the highest motives and best diction, servants with silver trays distributing sherry poured from cut glass decanters, a well-dressed corpse in a room locked from the inside, and no weapon in sight.

Sorry, not for me. I've read a few, but I don't make a habit of it, except for Agatha Christie's Hercule Poirot stories. I like Poirot because he's egotistical and slightly insane, not because he's in the best mystery stories. He's a good role model for me personally. By the way, did you know that Agatha hated him after a while? She even called him a "detestable, bombastic, tiresome, ego-centric little creep." But he made lots of money for her. You'd think she'd be more appreciative.

The cozy is a bit slower moving than today's popular styles. There are fewer bodies and they tend to be "discovered" rather than dropped through the skylight onto the banquet table as the host stands up to give a toast. The crime is usually a murder, but it's a genteel murder, and might even be inadvertently committed during the theft of a world famous diamond necklace.

I prefer more intensity in the stories I read, but cozies continue to be popular with other readers. Don't discount them.

Noir

Originally set in the poorly lighted back alleys of Paris and San Francisco, the noir style traces its origins to the gritty writing of Dashiell Hammett and his sleuth Sam Spade, and Raymond Chandler writing about his uncompromising private detective Phillip Marlowe. They set the style and tone, and we have evolved from those early days to the Mike Hammers, Peter Gunns, and Spensers of today.

These main characters wallow in the underworld or skirt its periphery. They are familiar with the sordid aspects of their communities, and they know and are known by the criminal players, even though they might not be direct participants in criminal deeds. The cops know them too, and are usually hassling them about something much more serious than outstanding parking tickets, although an occasional "honest" cop comes through for them when the chips are down.

The noir style is cynicism distilled. Humanity is evil. The protagonist might be the only "moral" character around, and even his moral stance is somewhat skewed by the bleak reality he swims in, like a shark who cleans up the ocean's garbage, and only eats a seal pup or a human child once in a while when he absolutely has to.

Legal Thriller

Catching the villain is one thing, but many people love the drama of the courtroom. John Grisham, an attorney himself, has made his literary career in this realm. Remember Perry Mason from that venerable television show? He always got his man (woman), too, usually on the witness stand in the closing moments of the show.

Michael Connelly's *Lincoln Lawyer* has been a huge success for him. His character is a wily defense attorney who will handle any criminal case that comes along, but only if the client has the cash up front to pay for his services. Much of the action occurs outside of the courtroom and the stories tend more toward character study and analysis than courtroom drama. I like this sort of thing for the complexity of the character interactions and the ethical questions that inevitably arise. Make no mistake about it, this is technical writing. There are people out there just waiting to pounce on your errors. And they will.

To write this type of a book, you need to have a solid understanding of the intricacies of criminal law, legal ethics, the rules of evidence, and courtroom procedure. You can't wing it. All the technical aspects have to be absolutely correct. It helps to have a legal education, and helps even more if you have years of experience in the legal system of the jurisdiction you write about.

I'm not saying that this genre is out of your league. There are non-lawyers who can write legal thrillers that hold readers' attention and which are factually and procedurally (!) correct. Can you do it? It might be worth a try, but it's not simple.

Don't despair. There are plenty of reference works out there to help. I find that I regularly refer to my *Black's Law Dictionary* and *North Carolina Crimes* for definitions and details, and once I have the basics, I hit the Internet for the intricacies.

Exercises – Legal Thriller

- Find a local attorney who will work with you to explain legal tactics and procedure.
- Go to court and sit through several calendar calls and trials.
- Have you ever sued someone or been sued? How did that make you feel? How did it affect your life and the people around you?
- If you are ever summoned for jury duty, go and serve. It's a free legal education.

Police Procedural

Cops, cops, and more cops. Think *Hill Street Blues*, *CSI*, or *NCIS*. If you're old enough, think *Dragnet*. Think forensics, and dogged footwork to track down innumerable leads, most of which are dead ends (pardon the pun), but at least one of which will lead to the pot of evidentiary gold at the end of a sinister rainbow.

Think departments vying for limited budget resources and fighting amongst themselves for mayoral notice. Think interactions between individual cops who've known one another for the years needed to build serious personal animosities. Think corrupt cops and the pressures on newbies to go with the flow of dirty systems on the take.

And of course, think about Lancelot, the knight in shining armor, newly arrived on the scene and determined to remain pure. Think Serpico, and the disastrous results of his trying to do the right thing in a system that has little tolerance for that kind of behavior. And let's not forget Popeye Doyle from *The French Connection*, a detective determined to reach the right results by all the wrong means if that's what is needed.

The king of this genre, for my money, is Ed

McBain. He wrote the 87th Precinct novels, in which several criminal plots wove through the book, most of which were solved by the end. These books provide a variety of police experiences and plots, several mysteries to solve within one book, many strange characters the police encounter, and great interactions between the police characters themselves who have to deal with one another shift to shift on their way from taking the initial call to closing their cases.

The inner workings of police departments fascinate readers. But the writer of this genre needs to have sources of technical information, and that means having a working relationship with the police department you're writing about. Many local public safety agencies stage what's popularly known as a Citizen's Police Academy. Check with your local police department. By going through this program, you won't be qualified to wear a badge, but you will learn much about the inner workings of your local department, including laws controlling search, seizure and arrest, first response protocols, crime scene investigation, firearms, and much more. For many of these academies, the climactic event is taking the class out to the firing range for some practical firearms exposure. Best of all, these programs are usually free to the public. (You might have to buy your own ammunition for the range event.)

Many departments, both city departments and far-ranging sheriff's or state police agencies, also have Ride Along programs. If you want to see what the officer on the street faces on a daily basis, sign up to ride. Several writers in my critique group have done this and had some interesting experiences to tell us about. Again, these programs are generally free to the public. Take advantage of them. It's your tax dollars at work.

Exercises – Police

- Find a local source for information on police policy and procedure. This might be the public relations office of your city or county public safety bureaus. Using the "six degrees of separation" principle, find links to law enforcement professionals you can approach directly for information and background material.
- Find out if your local city police or county sheriff's departments offer "ride along" programs. Many departments offer regular citizens learning opportunities such as this. Take a ride or two. Vary the seasons and times of day.
- For writers, the sought after jewel is the Citizens' Police Academy run by a law enforcement agency. If you can find such a program in your home town or nearby, sign up. These programs usually run for several weeks and will teach you how the department is organized and how the police do their work. You'll probably have a hands-on shooting experience on the police gun range, too.

Private Investigator – Hard-nosed or Otherwise

There are lots of PI characters. They range from the toughest of tough, Robert B. Parker's Spenser for example, to the vulnerable but wily female insurance investigator like Sue Grafton's Kinsey Millhone. They usually have personal issues ranging from the lousy childhoods that haunt them, to bad marriages and alcoholism.

A good fit for your PI is a former police officer or detective. For whatever reason, they've left the department. Perhaps they were asked to leave or were flat out fired. Regardless, their professional history brings with it knowledge of police policy and investigative procedure, along with tattered remnants of contacts within the police community. Those contacts can come in handy for the PI if they're positive, or if negative, they can be handy for the author in creating stumbling blocks for the protagonist.

Though not a licensed private investigator, Sherlock Holmes was the world's first "consulting detective." An interesting note is that although Sherlock Holmes made Sir Arthur Conan Doyle's fortune, Sir Arthur resented Holmes for his success and tried to kill the pipe-smoking, cocaine-using sleuth off. Sherlock's fans wouldn't stand for it. Sir Arthur wanted his other more serious writings to be what he became famous for, but it wasn't to be.

Exercises – PI

Note: For these exercises, don't rely on hearsay or a television series. The challenge is to find out the true facts of the situation.

- Find out what the requirements are to obtain a PI license in your state or jurisdiction.
- What are the limits on a PI's activities and authority?
- Can a PI make an arrest in your jurisdiction? Can a bounty hunter or skip tracer make an arrest in your jurisdiction? How does this work?
- What is a PI, bounty hunter, or skip tracer's legal liability?

Amateur Crime Solver

Many of today's popular mysteries feature an average citizen as the protagonist. This character is an ordinary person who gets swept up in other people's problems and has to find a way through to a solution. In real life, this individual is the least likely person to solve a crime, but . . . wrong place, wrong time, and there they are, right in the middle of a big literary mess.

Although many contemporary mysteries are solved by amateurs, these protagonists share several exceptional characteristics. They are inquisitive and tenacious by nature, and they are clever in unique ways. They are willing to take risks, or when the gauntlet is thrown down, they will to pick it up and crash onwards in the dark until circumstances and facts combine and they win the day. These are my favorite types of characters.

Your protagonist might be a busy-body like Miss Marple who continually sticks her nose into other folks' business. He or she might be an accountant or a pocket-protector type who doesn't even like mysteries. My own series character, Ben Bones, is a genealogist who gets called out on seemingly simple research jobs that become tangled webs when he discovers what people don't want found, or they decide they want what he finds for themselves alone and are willing to kill for it.

Exercises – Amateur Crime Solver

- List ten professions in which an amateur crime solver might encounter a crime to solve. Examples: tailor, shoe salesman, plumber, garage mechanic, hairdresser.
- What crimes might these people encounter and how might they be solved?
- List five characteristics (besides those I have listed above) which would help an amateur solve a crime.

Preferred Crimes - Best & Worst

First, let's categorize and identify crimes, then discuss various criminal motives. A word of advice here: get your legal definitions right.

Do you know the difference between a misdemeanor and a felony? Which is worse? According to *Black's Law Dictionary,* a misdemeanor is an "offense lower than felonies and generally those punishable by fine or imprisonment otherwise than in penitentiary." In most states and under federal law, a felony is "a crime of a graver or more serious nature," and which may be "punishable by death or imprisonment for a term exceeding one year." In most jurisdictions, imprisonment for a term greater than one year is the deciding factor. I don't know how a leap year count would influence your plot, but it might provide an interesting wrinkle. (Is it possible that a misdemeanor sentence of less than a year could inadvertently become a felony sentence of more than a year served? Could this change the operative definitions for your character? What are the legal ramifications for all concerned?)

I once received a synopsis from an aspiring writer which said that his character had recently completed 90 days in the state penitentiary? Really? And here I thought a 90-day sentence would be served in a county facility. From what he said about his story, I could only surmise that the character had been convicted of a felony rather than a misdemeanor, and the felony sentence had been reversed by a higher court or he'd been pardoned by the governor (for unspecified services rendered?). Perhaps this is an excusable error for a new writer, but not how things would work in the real world.

Maybe it could happen due to overcrowding in the county.

Crimes in the statutes are defined as combinations of specific elements. All of the elements must be present for the crime to meet its specifications. At trial, each element must be proven in court beyond a reasonable doubt. Lack of one element means that particular crime wasn't committed, although other ancillary charges might apply.

For example, in North Carolina, the crime of Misdemeanor Larceny is defined in the North Carolina General Statutes (14-72) as a Class 1 Misdemeanor. The property's value cannot exceed $1,000. Its elements are specifically listed as follows:

> 1. takes the personal property belonging to another
> 2. and carries it away
> 3. without the consent of the possessor, and
> 4. with the intent to deprive the possessor of its use permanently
> 5. knowing that the taker was not entitled to it.

At common law, robbery is face-to-face, usually includes violence or the threat of violence, and can occur at any time day or night. Common law burglary happens at night and usually involves entry into a dwelling place with felonious intent. Check the state laws for the venue where your crime is committed. There's nothing worse than a factual mistake that a reader catches you on. It's a severe blow to your credibility. This topic is discussed further in the section on research.

An interesting point that many mystery writing teachers miss revolves around the charging of crimes. In real life, it's rare that a single charge is levied against an individual. The authorities like to pile them on. Sometimes the charges are all legitimate. Sometimes they're added solely in the hope of a later plea bargain on one or two of the charged offenses and a dismissal of the others in exchange for the plea. This is real life in many jurisdictions. Call your local district attorney or public defender offices and ask about this. Use it to enrich (complicate) your character's dilemmas.

And don't forget about charging your characters with conspiracy. When the authorities need a catch-all crime to bargain with, conspiracy is a favorite. If two or more people plan an illegal act and have the intent to do it, that's a conspiracy. They don't have to actually do anything. They don't have to buy their lock picks, balaclavas, or weapons. All they have to do is plan to do it and they're guilty, or at least chargeable.

Crimes Against Persons

Homicide

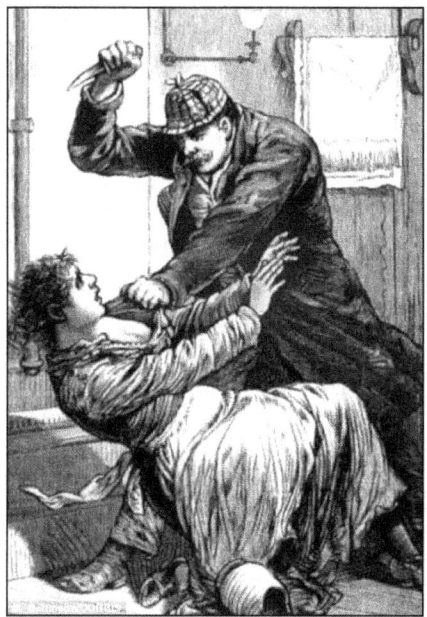

Murder is the crime of first resort for writers. It's been many mystery writer's darling since the earliest days of our craft. After all, what better proof is there that a crime has been committed than a bloody corpse hanging from a chandelier or a bag full of miscellaneous body parts stinking up a dumpster?

But be clear that all homicides are not murders. There are accidental deaths, too, as in auto accidents. If it's done on purpose, with malice aforethought or with a depraved heart, it's murder. If it's an accident, it's still death, but it might be manslaughter.

Many murderers complicate things by trying

to hide the murder. They try to disguise the deed by making it look like an accident. Some might succeed in real life, though rarely, but they never succeed in your stories, do they?

In all homicide cases, a human being must have died, and problems inherent in the death drive your story. Not only do we have to find out who did it, where, and by what method, (Colonel Ketchup in the upstairs bath with the pipe wrench?), but why did they do it? Was it revenge? Was it to remove an obstacle to another plan? Was it to cover up another crime? Was the death an unintended accident (or necessity) in the course of perpetrating a very different nefarious act? The plot can easily thicken from a thin broth to a viscous gruel.

Murder, though absolute, comes in varying degrees: first degree, second degree, voluntary manslaughter, and involuntary manslaughter. Some states, such as North Carolina where I live, also have two classes of death by vehicle: felony or misdemeanor. Which one is charged depends on whether impaired driving was involved or not.

| Death by Category ||||
Category	State of Mind	Possible Elements	Possible Sentence
1st Degree	Intent to kill.	Malice aforethought. Premeditation (planned). Ambush.	Death. Life imprisonment.
2nd Degree	No intent. Indifference to human life.	No premeditation. Depraved heart.	Death. Life Imprisonment (with or without parole).
Felony Murder	Other crime.	Killing in course of other felony.	Same as above.
Manslaughter			
Voluntary Manslaughter	No intent or malice. Accident.		Term of years (varies by jurisdiction).
Involuntary Manslaughter	Reckless behavior.		
Justifiable	Self defense or defense of another.		May not be charged.

Exercises – Homicide

- List ten motives for murder. Feel free to use emotional responses to events in your own life. You can even play out the murder that you didn't or wouldn't commit, but had seriously thought to carry out. Bury the next door neighbor, chop up the classmate who stole your boyfriend, poison your spouse, shoot your ex. Get the idea?
- Think of five workable methods to kill another human being. Examples: shooting, poisoning, strangulation. Be creative. You never know when you'll

really need this information. It will help if you've thought it out beforehand.
- Think of five realistic ways to dispose of a corpse. Examples: acid bath, cement overshoes, burying in the woods, feeding to sharks, the ever popular wood chipper.

Robbery

You might not think so initially because stealing property is involved, but most criminal codes classify robbery as a crime against a person. This is because it involves a threat of physical violence if the swag isn't handed over.

Unless you're writing for television or the criminal is a serial robber, this crime may not be enough in itself. In many instances, the robbery attempt will result in an inadvertent or unplanned murder. This is great for the novelist and provides the propulsion needed into a longer and more involved story.

I remember being robbed at gunpoint on the street one summer's evening while walking my girl home from a date. Something seemed wrong about the two guys on the other side of the street. I couldn't state it succinctly, but it seemed as though they were tracking us, staying parallel to us and not ahead or behind. Finally they crossed the street and, in the shade of a live oak tree, one of them pointed a huge revolver at me and told me to throw my wallet on the ground. I never kept money in my wallet, just my driver's license and such, and I told him so. He got agitated and repeated his demand to throw it on the ground. I dug out the folded three dollars left over from my big date, and dropped it in front of him. He waved us off and we ran for it.

That was my firsthand experience with robbery. It was also my last robbery experience to date. That's okay, too. I don't need more of that level of threat or excitement. I have also been burgled, but that's considered a crime against property.

Assault and Battery

Assault and battery are often spoken of in a single phrase by non-lawyers, but in many jurisdictions they are very different crimes.

At common law, an assault is only the threat to do physical harm to another person. It may or may not involve a weapon. There may be no actual contact with the intended victim, but if the victim perceives the threat as real, or is put in fear, an assault has occurred. Check your state statutes.

In North Carolina, child abuse is classed as an assault, whether it's simple abuse, inflicting serious injury, child prostitution, or sexual acts.

Rape is a sexual assault and it may be classified separately and specifically in your state. In many cases, it is a power crime. North Carolina deals with different degrees of rape depending on whether force or a weapon was used, or if the rape was on a person between 12 and 13 years of age. Read your state statutes carefully. Interview a rape investigator or prosecutor if you can.

At common law, and in many states, battery is the touching of another person without that person's consent. A strike to the head with a blunt instrument is a battery. But an innocent peck on the cheek is also a battery if the kiss was without consent. Can you imagine such a thing? But that's the law. (A favorite law school aphorism is: "The law is an ass.")

In my first semester of law school, no one would touch anyone else after that first class on battery. Sensitivity suddenly ran high with our new knowledge. People were afraid to ask someone out on a date for fear of an "unconsented touching." That would be a battery, and we all were trying to keep our noses extremely clean because of the bar examiners.

Exercises – Assault and/or Battery

- Were you ever assaulted? Battered? Explain in two short paragraphs.
- What did you experience emotionally at the time? Later?
- Did you ever want to commit a battery? What were the circumstances? Did you come to your senses beforehand or did you go ahead with your plan? Either way, what was the result?

Human Trafficking - Kidnapping, Slavery, Illegal Immigration

I don't have experience in these areas. I don't want experience in these areas. However, authorities take these things rather seriously. With all the talk these days about immigration, legal and illegal, that might be a great theme for this political moment. Next year, perhaps other themes will demand our attention.

Crimes Against Property

Conversion (Theft)

Conversion simply means taking another person's property for one's own use. The criminal is converting it from the rightful owner's possession and use to his.

This type of crime is the classic. It's based in a simple profit motive. At least it seems to be unless it's a mask, a misdirection to steer your protagonist away from the real, and usually more serious, crime. And the perpetrating character can be as obvious or devious as you want to imagine him or her.

The crime can be as simple as stealing the air pump off the neighbor kid's bicycle. It might be confrontational, as when the schoolyard bully demands his victim's lunch money. Or it might reach the level of a dictator's ripping off the oil and diamond wealth of his country for 20 years before being deposed and hung by his ankles from a lamppost or retiring to the south of France to live in luxury.

Besides the traditional confrontational robbery, conversion can be perpetrated by fraud or trickery.

Too many people want to take advantage of a "good deal" when it's presented, and they don't look beyond the obvious. How about the paving company that sells a shoddy asphalt job to the aged widow down the street, with a cash payment in front of course? "We've got this asphalt left over from a job we just completed and it's a shame to waste it, but cash payment is our policy, ma'am."

There are many subtle frauds possible. "Theft by trick" is a common named crime on the statute books of many states. Here's a partial list: insurance frauds, obtaining money by stating "facts" that are untrue, welfare and food stamp frauds, Medicare fraud, various computer frauds and manipulations, and the highest form of the conversion artist's craft: forged or counterfeit documents.

You might build a story around a perfectly legal "crime" like establishing off-shore shell companies that make tracking the flow of funds nearly impossible. Some people might even think there's a moral (if not legal) question to a lawyer's fee of a third of the jury's award to a mangled industrial accident victim.

There's infinite variation possible with conversion. Remember Woody Guthrie's famous line, "Some will rob you with a six-gun, and some with a fountain pen." It's your book and you can do almost (!) anything you want in it.

Burglary

At common law, burglary is defined as entering (usually by breaking and entering, which might be a separate charge) a building or structure, at night, with the intention of committing a felony. Some states divide the crime into first, second, or third degrees, usually on the basis of whether the building or sleeping space was occupied or not. Interestingly, an affirmative defense against the charge in some jurisdictions is that the structure had been abandoned.

An odd twist in North Carolina is the crime of "breaking out of a dwelling." If the criminal entered without consent and then has to break out, he might be convicted of this Class D felony and could serve 12 to 40 years imprisonment.

In many states, mere possession of burglary

tools such as lock picks or a crowbar is itself a crime. The tools might be circumstantial evidence if only in the trunk of a car. If the tools are in a bag in the suspect's hands when he/she is in the alley behind a closed store at night and carrying a weapon at the time. . . that's more probative.

Exercises – Robbery & Burglary

- In a couple of paragraphs, describe any time you were robbed or burgled. What were the circumstances? What was your immediate reaction? How did you feel hours later? Were there lingering fears or other emotions? How did officials react?

Blackmail & Extortion

Blackmail is possible when the bad guy has

damaging or embarrassing information about a recognized and revered pillar of the community, a politician, or a religious leader.

Were they in the army together when atrocities were performed? Did they grow up in the same neighborhood and become members of the same or rival gangs? Was the one seen doing something that the other now threatens to tell the world all about? Maybe what starts out as an extortion story flips around to become murder to ensure that the secret remains a secret.

What does the blackmailer really want? Is this about power, is it just about the money, or is it something more nefarious? Perhaps he/she requires the victim to perform some act or service which will, in the end, entangle the victim even deeper in the perp's web. I don't know. Since it's your story; you'll have to figure it out.

Drug Crimes

There are many different types of drug crimes. Some drug crimes can provide fodder for a novel's plot; others don't lend themselves to such a high purpose. Drugs can equate to big money involving large sums of cash, and that's great motivation for criminals.

Drug crimes worth pursuing can involve drug cartels, the manufacture of drugs, international intrigues, smuggling by relatively naïve "mules" or in dope-filled planes, money laundering, bribery of politicians and law enforcement officials, huge marijuana farming operations or small scale organic growers; the list goes on and on. These crimes might even be called "crimes against civilization." To find a worthwhile drug crime, follow the money.

Although fallen and down-and-out characters are interesting as people and useful to the writer, street level drug crimes generally aren't substantial enough to support a plot by themselves. There isn't enough money involved, even though there might be plenty of human interest. But if you tend to write stories that are psychological in nature, this might be a good gutter for you to wallow in.

Street level drug crimes can be used as a focal point of gang violence, for person-to-person revenge, or as a teaser to lead your characters along a devious track to the ever invisible and well insulated "Mr. Big." Remember Charles Bronson's *Death Wish* films in which he played a vengeful vigilante? The unplanned murder of character Paul Kersey's wife and daughter during a home break-in provided the impetus for a popular movie series. It showed something of the public's outrage, didn't it? If you sense a groundswell of public sentiment, you might be able to use it to propel your own plot. Read the newspaper occasionally. There's a great deal of raw material there.

Arson

In North Carolina, arson is divided into two degrees of seriousness, depending on whether the building was occupied or not. It's easy enough to understand why.

For our writing purposes, the arson may not be the primary crime. Ask why the arsonist's target was chosen? Look for prior relationships between the involved parties. Even where the reason for the arson is obscure, there might be historical animosities at work. Find them. Maybe the crime has a political motive. How about a religious motive, as in cleansing by fire?

As in real life, arson might be used as a secondary crime to conceal the primary and more serious crime, such as an attempt to destroy a corpse or other evidence of murder. This is rarely successful these days because of advances in forensic science. If your story is set at an earlier time in the history of criminality, the perp might get away with it. Who knows? It's your job as a writer to make that happen, but please pay attention to the science of the time. Get it right.

Money Laundering

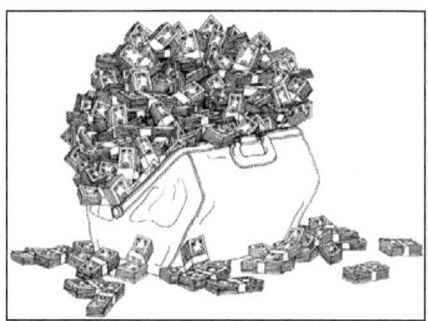

I've made this a separate area of criminal endeavor because it's evolved into its own industry. In the old days, money laundering meant carrying a suitcase of cash from where it was gathered over to a legitimate business where it could appear as cash income. No longer.

Money laundering has become a sophisticated, white collar crime that makes use of international banks, off-shore numbered accounts, shell corporations, straw man real estate deals, high level financial skills and manipulations, and the like. Don't ask me for details because it's too complicated for me to understand. I'm still thinking at the level of pockets full of dimes and quarters. In my real life I've been accused of not thinking big enough, and I guess it's true. This is just one example.

Having said that though, for writers with more financial sophistication than yours truly, those who need their cash income cleaned up, and those who launder the illegally obtained money can provide an array of interesting and devious characters and intrigues on both sides of the law. Sometimes the "good guys" are as bad as the crooks; they just happen to be on the side that supports civilization instead of undermining it.

Sex Crimes

Prostitution

Prostitution is purported to be the oldest profession. Wherever there are humans, sexual services are a salable commodity. This has been true since forever. It's in our nature.

Nonetheless, in most places, prostitution and soliciting for prostitution are considered detrimental to an orderly society and have been written into the law as punishable crimes. Advances in birth control, prophylaxis, and treatment of sexually transmitted disease haven't changed the situation.

Prostitution is the business of sex, and is defined as the offering or receiving of the body for sexual intercourse for hire.

It's been said that sex makes the world go 'round. I believe this, but this is another area where I'm just too naïve to understand all the subtleties. Regardless of my ignorance and lack of experience, there are enough horny people in the world to make the sex trade a huge opportunity for criminal activity.

The hands-on practitioners of honey-pot

skills aren't the only ones involved. Don't forget those folks who manage the services of prostitutes and pornographers for others.

In North Carolina, assignation is also a crime. Assignation in this context means making an appointment to engage in prostitution or making arrangements for prostitution. A "john" or "trick" (a prostitute's customer) or a street level pimp (a prostitute's business manager) would be guilty of this crime, whether the sexual service was provided or not. The pimps, the organized crime businessmen, the taxi drivers who know where to find local action for the visiting traveling salesman, and the hotel clerks who turn a blind eye for an extra ten bucks are all criminals, too.

In the "art" world, let's not neglect the filmmakers, actors and actresses, the store front porno shops, and the online sellers. I guess 900 number telephone sex would fit into this category, too. They're acting, aren't they?

Even if there are people who won't get involved physically, there are those who like to watch. Personally, I think doing is more fun and satisfying than merely watching. But films and books of a sexual nature continue to proliferate, and the market for these productions continues to increase. This genre may prove to be your best opportunity to break the publication barrier. Here's some free business advice from yours truly: use a pen name.

A word about pedophilia, the sexual exploitation of children. As far as I'm concerned, adults can do what they want to and with whomever they want, if all those involved agree. But to destroy a child's sense of innocence, to destroy their trust, to poison a young mind and body, and to create the sex criminal of the future into the bargain . . . I find this horribly distasteful. Am I being old fashioned? Am I letting my prejudice show? Sure. I'm entitled to my opinions.

As much as I dislike the idea of pedophilia itself, I dislike even more when adults take advantage of a position of power or trust to perpetrate sexual crimes on children. We've heard much in recent years about pederast priests, coaches, and scout leaders who are sexual predators. This is not just inappropriate behavior on their parts. It's the worst sort of behavior, and these folks often get what they richly deserve when caught, convicted, and incarcerated. Even the most vicious criminals don't condone that sort of behavior.

But having voiced my opinion, I believe there are stories to be written on this subject, too. If you have the stomach for it, go ahead.

Criminal Miscellany

Criminal Motives

I'm not a trained psychologist, but I am a habitual observer of people and their antics. As a writer of believable fiction, you must become an astute observer of human behavior, too. You need to grow antennae that pop up and twitch when you come across cupidity, maliciousness, or even simple stupidity in your fellow humans. Antennae become more sensitive with time and use; they rarely wear out from sensing over however many years.

People commit crimes for various reasons. Some reasons may seem justifiable in the perpetrator's mind, but a distinction should be made between motive and intent. Motive may be the reason for a crime, but motive is not an element that must be proven. Intent is the determination to do the deed, and that is an element of many a defined crime that must be proven in court. Motive might be interesting to observers and analysts, but in the eyes of the law, a crime is a crime, offending both individuals and society as a whole, and it must be dealt with as such regardless of whether a motive is clear, vague, or entirely lacking.

Sometimes a finger is pointed at the empty bottle on the table. The excuse for the antisocial behavior might be, "The booze made me do it." I have a theory about that, about alcohol and drugs, that is. They don't "make" anyone do anything that they wouldn't have done if there were no societal restraint, or no legal prohibition against that particular behavior. Alcohol and drugs seem to only release the inner person and the tendencies which were there all the time. A possible exception to this theory is the addict who is in true physical need of a fix and steals and sells something to get the money to buy the drug.

Sheer stupidity may be a factor as well. I'm not talking here about people with the disability of low intelligence. Statistically speaking, intelligence is distributed along a bell curve, and not everyone is on the high end. These people might get into trouble simply because they lack information or don't think things through.

Many people don't consider the consequences of their actions. Maybe they weren't taught how to think ahead. Others, the sociopaths and psychopaths amongst us, just don't care. You've undoubtedly met some of these "special" people in your own lives. They might not make good characters for your writing because they're too shallow. On the other hand, they might be exactly the uber-criminal you need, if they can be portrayed as clever enough.

Profit (Greed)

In our capitalist western culture, everybody

is chasing a buck. That's probably true all over the world, whatever the culture. The one who has the most (dollars, shekels, camels, goats, toys, etc.) gets the girl. Some folks will go to extreme lengths to get that extra camel.

There are many ways to profit, from simple thefts to devious white collar crimes, from the overt stick-up on the street at gunpoint to the subtle business contract full of tricky clauses.

As I read the never ending news reports of corruption and thievery in the real world, I always wonder exactly how much money is enough. If you have a million, how many more millions do you need to be satisfied? If you have a billion, well, the question becomes moot, at least to me. But there are some people who will never have enough. Perhaps it's the acquiring that's the thrill, and not the possession. Maybe it's the power of being able to dominate an opponent. Maybe they didn't get enough mother's milk as babies. Who knows?

But there are people at the lower end of the thieving scale too: the waiter who short changes a customer for the extra $1 tip; the corporate accountant who has a secret account he shunts money to when doing the company books; the computer programmer who collects the odd .00001 from his boss's sales; the dentist's receptionist who embezzles her boss's thousands instead of making the expected bank deposits. And what about Jean Valjean of *Les Misérables* fame who stole a loaf of bread to feed his starving family? Is theft ever justified? Can theft ever be classified as highly motivated? What about stealing the plans for the invasion of your country by your bordering enemy?

Moral questions aside, profit is a great motivator for fictional crime as well as real world crime. For me, simple greed is the Grand Motive.

Power

Power is a tricky motivation. Several identified reasons for power crimes are:

1. To obtain power – For example, when a powerless person seeks to assert themselves over others by threats of violence. "Do this or else!"

A clause in a will that demands certain behavior of a named beneficiary or the bequest will be revoked is known as an "in terrorem clause."

2. To demonstrate power – Proving that one has power over another might be accomplished through a kidnapping event, or ongoing blackmail.

3. To maintain power – Ongoing blackmail might serve to prove that one has continuing power over the victim. The schoolyard bully also wants to keep others subjugated to his will.

4. To re-acquire lost power – This might occur when a person no longer has influence over others, as when a deposed leader tries to take over again. Napoleon Bonaparte is a prime historical example of this.

I have never wanted power. I'm not comfortable being in a position of power. Too much responsibility. It's too easy to take advantage of people who have less power or less knowledge. Perhaps I suspect that the temptation might be too strong for me and my high moral stance would evaporate into memory.

There are people who want as much power as they can get. I don't understand the motivation. But motivation aside, it's their acts toward others that make a plot sing. It might be the dictator of a small country who uses his police or military to kill off his opposition. It might be a school principal who has no power in his marriage or business relationships and becomes a ranting tyrant and child beater in his professional role. It might be the restaurateur who lords it over his kitchen and wait staff. It might be Hitler or Noriega, or it might be the picked-on kid next door who throws rocks at squirrels or kicks the family dog.

I don't expect to ever write a power story. I don't understand the motivation well enough. Maybe after I earn a doctorate in psychology.

Revenge

The Roman poet Juvenal is quoted for saying, "Revenge is a dish best served cold." I wouldn't know. Maybe I'm not quite human, but I've never sought revenge. I consider it a rather infantile approach to problem solving between humans.

But there are numerous cultures and a great many individuals in the world who believe in revenge. Many times it's a question of "honor" to them or their families. Blood feuds, Hatfields and McCoys type situations, can be found all over the planet. In some cultures, life without seeking revenge is a life without honor.

Vengeful people can wait for years to get the upper hand on an opponent or colleague who bested them in the past. This can be a strong motivation in a business drama. Politics can be a hotbed for revenge, too, though saner people will go forward in their lives instead of obsessing about past injustices, real or imagined.

Love

In my life, love isn't a sufficient motive for much of anything. I'm too cynical about relationships and don't know how to do them well. No one ever taught me how.

I remember sitting in my car at 3 A.M. one night thinking terrible thoughts, watching the dark windows in a buddy's apartment, my soon-to-be ex-girlfriend's car parked outside with its engine cold. Love as a motive? No. But jealousy? Oh, baby, now that's a motive. I came to my senses after a while of sitting and stewing. I wrote the situation off as one I couldn't change, tossed the length of 2x4 out of my car window, and drove home to a solitary bed.

But there are people in the world who don't have the same level of insight (cynicism?) as me, and I'm sure there are people who will kill for love and its insane sibling jealousy. How that helps their courting, I can't imagine. Maybe it demonstrates the depth of their commitment, if not their hormonal imbalance. Maybe a lover demands a criminal act of the significant other as proof of the professed love.

I don't know. I'm just throwing questions out here, I don't have answers.

Thousands of mystery stories have been

written on the theme of love. I might write one myself sometime. But I'll warn you now not to read it. It's bound to ruin your positive attitude.

Misc. Motives

Sometimes the motivation for a criminal act is simple pride or stupidity. For example, there was a shooting in my neighborhood recently because of a bicycle theft. A kid stole a bike from another kid and when the victim's father went to get his son's bike back, the thief's father shot and killed him. Would you do that? For a bicycle? I wouldn't. But I sure would write about it.

Young perpetrators might commit a crime on a dare or simply for the thrill of it. Adrenalin is a powerful drug that we produce in our own bodies. It can be highly addictive and may support a pattern of behavior that lasts into adulthood and requires higher and higher levels of thrill to attain the sought-for high. Where do daredevils come from?

In these days of intense religious belief, perpetrators may act to cleanse the world of sinners, to precipitate religious conflicts between groups, or to force belief on unbelievers. A religiously motivated act may sometimes be difficult to distinguish from a purely political act.

Hate crimes are crimes aimed at a particular group rather than at specific individuals. The victim is an anonymous individual member of that group. Hate against a group might result from a twisted view of an incident in the perpetrator's past, or it might be a family artifact passed down through the generations as part of the perpetrator's upbringing. A bumper sticker I saw said "Hate is a family value." This is true in some families.

One excuse that is heard over and over again in court is, "The liquor made me do it." That's simple nonsense. I believe that alcohol simply lowers your inhibitions and lets your true nature reveal itself.

Drugs are another matter. Addictive drugs create a physical need that must be satisfied. The body demands to have the chemical onboard. With heroin and other opiates there is little the addict can do to block this need except to go through a painful withdrawal process, which they tend to avoid. To prevent the agony of withdrawal, the perpetrator does things he/she would not ordinarily do in order to obtain more of the drug.

As for methamphetamine and its relatives, as I understand it, they are physically and psychologically addictive.

Hallucinogens aren't physically addictive, nor is marijuana, although some anti-drug zealots might argue the point.

Manner, Cause & Mechanism of Death

Autopsy

An autopsy is done to determine the facts surrounding a death. Autopsies are performed for a variety of reasons and by a variety of people, depending on the rules of your jurisdiction. In many urban areas, trained pathologists are the people who perform autopsies. In areas with fewer resources, the person doing the autopsy might be a medical doctor, a lab technician, perhaps even a mortician.

An autopsy examines each organ of the body in detail. Time of death can be established by measuring body temperature, or by analysis of the stomach contents and their stage of digestion. Insect remains in or on a found corpse can sometimes help determine time and place of death.

Pathologists are concerned with three important things: the manner of death, the cause, and the mechanism. If your story demands a death, you need to consider these things, too. They may be the key to structuring your story and solving the crime.

Manner of Death

Manner of death breaks into five categories:
- Natural - Death occurred due to disease, old age, or other natural causes. Death may occur at home or in hospice or hospital. There is usually no suspicion of foul play.

- Homicide - The death was caused by another person, whether premeditated, felony murder, or manslaughter.
- Suicide - The deceased person killed themselves one way or another.
- Accident - Death occurred due to unforeseen circumstances, or by what is known as misadventure. Example of famous last words: "Hey, you guys, watch this!"
- Undetermined - You can guess what this means, can't you?

Cause of Death

What was the specific reason for the death? Was it cancer, heart attack, strangulation, auto accident, a lightning strike, or a broken neck from falling off a ladder? Each cause of death will show as physiological changes in the body. Thus, a skilled pathologist can often determine the exact cause of death.

Mechanism of Death

What caused the cessation of life? Here are a few examples:
- If there was a shooting, the victim might have died from loss of blood. That would be the mechanism of death.
- In a car accident, the mechanism of death might be pulmonary arrest or impact damage that destroyed the brain.
- Cardiac arrhythmia might kill in a drug overdose.

Weapons

Weapons are part of the world of crime. In the England of past years, there were so-called "gentlemen" burglars. They considered themselves professionals and didn't carry weapons. Neither did the police. It's a different game now, and the police regularly find themselves outgunned by heavily armed bad guys. The criminal without a weapon is working at a disadvantage these days.

When you think "weapon," you might first think of a gun or knife, but don't limit yourself. There are as many varieties of weapons as there are situations where they might be used. If the criminal doesn't start out with a weapon, the nearest object at hand might be employed. Think of the housebreaker discovered in mid-crime who grabs a table lamp to club a screaming housewife. You as author need to be as opportunistic as your villains.

An author needs to choose weapons and use them correctly. This requires that you do your own research or that you have a knowledgeable consultant who will help you out. Don't guess at what a weapon will do or not do. There are nit-picking weapons experts out in the world who will read your book and are waiting to pounce on your weapon errors.

If you're planning for your villain to use a gun, consult your expert to find out if it's the appropriate gun for the job. It might not be. You can't kill someone at half a mile with a revolver. Go find the recommended type of gun somewhere. Examine its mechanisms, heft it in your hand with and without bullets, fire it if possible. Learn about it. Your writing will be better for the experience, and you won't be at risk of losing credibility with your readers.

Types of Weapons

These categories are somewhat arbitrary by necessity. Some items clearly belong in only one category, but others can be classified in several categories depending on how they are used.

- Projectile - Anything that throws something is a projectile weapon. They can also be classed as ranged weapons. Pistols, rifles, shotguns, spear guns, a thrown spear or javelin, even an atlatl (look it up). How about a thrown rock? Or a Chinese throwing star?
- Stabbing - Knife, spear (wielded by hand and not thrown), a reinforcing rod sticking out of concrete. A butter knife or screwdriver can be a stabbing weapon in the right (wrong?) hand. A pool cue can be used for either stabbing or clubbing (blunt instrument) depending of which end is used to inflict the damage.
- Blunt Instrument - A club or bludgeon, a policeman's baton, a tire iron, or the above-mentioned table lamp all qualify as blunt instruments. A thrown rock might be a projectile, but a rock held in the hand and used for hitting is definitely a bludgeon. How about knuckledusters (brass knuckles)?
- Poison - Can be fast-acting, like cyanide, or slow and administered over a long time. Poisoning is sometimes spoken of as a chemical insult to the body's systems. How about the radioactive element polonium ingested by the victim?

Exercises – Personal Criminal Experiences

- This is a writing exercise. I am not

interested in learning your personal history. I am interested in getting you to examine your experiences and your emotions connected with those experiences. Do this analysis for yourself. It will give you insights that will improve your writing.
- In several paragraphs, describe any time you were arrested and went to jail, whether for an overnight stay or for years of incarceration. How did the experience affect you? How did it affect other people in your life?
- If you haven't been arrested, how did you feel when a cop stopped you for a minor vehicle violation?

Writing Your Mystery

Words as tools

It's been said that the pen is mightier than the sword. I believe that the word is mightier than the chain saw, and that it can be wielded more precisely than the scalpel. Mark Twain said, "The difference between the right word and the almost right word is the difference between the lightning and the lightning bug." I couldn't have said it better myself.

When I was a kid, there was definitely something wrong with me. Call me a geek or a nerd, whatever your favorite appellation, but I used to read *Roget's Thesaurus* for fun. Geek? I'll accept that, but today, my vocabulary is strong and I am rarely at a loss for the precise word I need. I didn't enjoy practicing law for the few years I did that to people, but I did enjoy being able to use my entire vocabulary. I could speak and write as precisely as I wanted. After all, many of the folks I dealt with didn't understand what I was talking about anyway.

Words are not precious; they are tools for

clear communication. Thus, they must be chosen carefully and used judiciously. Just as too much salt can ruin a gourmet dish, so can too many words ruin what might have been an eloquent and pointed piece of writing. Remember that extremely important quote from Mark Twain. And then there was Ernest Hemingway, who was known for the preciseness of his writing. There was nothing extraneous in his prose. Every word served his purpose. He was a lean writer.

Blaise Pascal, the 17th-century French philosopher and mathematician, is quoted for saying, "I have made this letter longer than usual, only because I have not had time to make it shorter" (a possible paraphrase). Precision in writing takes time and great care.

Having cited these literary diamonds, I must now add my own coal to the pile. Write leanly. Chop ruthlessly. Be specific in your writing and avoid repeating the same thought in different words. Do not pad your writing to satisfy the word counting monster. If you get paid by the word, well, that's a temptation to be sure, but I'd rather be reprinted for the excellence of my writing and paid again and again for a high quality piece than become known for a bloated, garrulous writing style. You have the same choice.

Sources of ideas

Where does one go to find ideas for mysteries? There are lots of places. Start with real life. Look at your relatives, friends, and neighbors. Maybe even open a newspaper. The world is full of folks trying to take advantage of other people. This has been going on since the beginning of mankind. War, sexual competition, and getting the upper hand over others may be some of our most human attributes. Even chimpanzees do it. They have hierarchical order in their troupes. Depressing, eh? Maybe, but it provides rich raw material for any crime or mystery writer.

You might turn to *News of the Weird* or *The Darwin Awards* if you're looking for the ridiculous in human behaviors. What people actually attempt to do in real life is beyond the poor imagination of us so-called creative writers. In fact, your plot may be too absurd if you use this material. Who would believe it?

And of course, there's your own experience and imagination. If you have a background in police work, law, medicine, insurance, car repair, restaurant work, or virtually any other area of human endeavor, there's material to be mined there. Situations that demonstrate one human trying to get the better of another, to get revenge, to profit from another's misfortune, to manipulate the rules that govern behavior, abound in all professions.

Does this sound too cynical for you? Unfortunately, it's the way of the world. Want proof? Open your eyes wide and look around you. I'm not saying that everyone is a bad person. Far from it. But this is your opportunity to take advantage of the evil that abounds instead of being an unknowing victim.

What's nice about being a writer is that you don't have to compromise your higher ideals or morals. You can do it all in your head and on paper. Steal. Embezzle. Get revenge. Murder your spouse, your children, your in-laws, your boss, your co-workers, your neighbors, the bully from elementary school, and bury them all in the back yard next to the family cat. And have fun while doing it. Maybe even make a profit from it. And you never have to hurt a soul.

Let's stop and think about this for a second. What exactly is your subject matter? Is it the bullet which races from the barrel of a gun and leaves a corpse on the floor? Is it the six thousand dollars embezzled from the church welfare fund to make a sure investment in crack cocaine? Or are you writing about a devious revenge that happens twenty years later for a real or imagined slight?

I don't think your story is about any of those things. Those might be the mechanisms of your story, but they're not the substance.

Your story must be about the people involved. I say "must" with great emphasis. Sure, you can work out a clever plot with all sorts of turnarounds and catches, with lots of red herrings thoroughly mixed up with legitimate clues, but if your readers aren't interested in the people in your story, clever doesn't matter a bit. Without human interest, you might as well be writing a forensics textbook.

People and human nature are your subject matter.

Characters

General suggestions

Characters have to be real. At least they must seem to be real to your readers. That means they can't be two-dimensional, can't be all good or all bad, can't be the classic cardboard cutout that we get so much writing advice about avoiding.

Characters can be found in a variety of flavors: realistic or fantastic, likeable or unlikable, emotionally flat or histrionic, skilled or inept, insightful or oblivious, benign or murderous, or with any other characteristics (or lack thereof) that you can imagine. The trick is to make them real enough that your readers believe in them and accept that their actions flow naturally from the personalities you've constructed for them. This is sometimes difficult, but it can be done. It must be done, and done by you, the writer.

Who is your character? What motivates him or her? What scars do they have on the outside, and equally or perhaps more importantly, what internal scars? Where did they get those scars, how and why? What is the character's back story, their history, their personal and business successes and failures, their crashed love affairs? What has Life done to them?

If you met the character in real life, what would you think about him or her? Here are a few choices for you to consider:

- This guy's a phony.
- This guy's too good to be true.
- A criminal type from head to toe.
- Mr. Wonderful.
- Ugly on the outside but with a beautiful soul.
- Beautiful on the outside but evil through and through.
- This guy is a didactic prig who I don't want anything to do with.
- This guy would make a wonderful stranger.

One of my most horrific writing experiences occurred when I made the terrible mistake of getting a series character's history wrong in subsequent books. It cost me hours of anguished rewriting and hundreds of dollars in reprinting, not to mention the embarrassment of having my gaffe pointed out to me by a detail-oriented reader or two.

The lesson I learned from that experience: develop and write out your character's complete back story. Write his/her entire life, from being dropped on his/her head as a baby all the way through stealing bubble gum from the neighborhood candy store, the disastrous high school prom, their first drunk, dropping out of college, smoking (but not inhaling), early employment, being fired from that first job that they hated anyway, traffic tickets, first sexual experiences (if any), and every personality quirk that's resulted as a consequence of those adventures. In short, know your character inside and out.

And then, don't file that history away. Keep it where it's easily accessible and can be referred to again and again. You're going to have to justify your character's actions and decisions from time to time, and that detailed history is where that motivation is generated.

Minor characters have a place, too. Don't ignore them, but don't make caricatures of them either. Who are they, what do they want, and what part do they play in the overall plot scheme? These are important questions.

I advise you to write back stories for your minor characters, too. Don't neglect this step. These personal histories don't need to be as extensive as your main character's, but they will give flesh to your characters in your mind, and thus through your writing to your readers.

Minor characters can be assistants, henchmen (henchpersons?), romantic interests, foils, sounding boards, spear carriers, or simply innocent bystanders. They might play larger or smaller roles, might appear in one scene and never again. They might be a red herring perp. They might turn out to be interesting enough to become a protagonist in your next story.

Sources for Characters

Where do we writers get our characters?

Writers are notorious vampires. We suck the life out of life, digest it, and then construct new life, new characters, from our digested material. We create fictional characters from the people we encounter in everyday life.

Remember Uncle Carl, the cigar smoking irritant who told dirty jokes at grandpa's funeral? Remember that guy you took a picture of on the street who then threatened you with those absolutely empty convict's eyes? Remember your favorite cousin Willy who stole the family treasure one day and disappeared over the horizon never to be seen again or even to be mentioned in family discussions? These people are the raw material of your new fictional world. Synthesize your characters from them.

As writers, we must be constant observers of the people around us. Sure, we see their clothing, their worn out shoes, their odd haircuts and physical characteristics, but it must go deeper than that. We need to study the behavior of the humans around us. Watch their mannerisms, their habits, their foibles, their good and bad points, the helpful or catastrophic decisions they make. Above all, observe their interactions with one another. At bottom, that's what our stories must talk about: human interaction and the disasters caused by those interpersonal tangles.

Clashing Opposites

It should be clear why you must have a problem solving protagonist hero and an evil bad guy. One is as important as the other. These two opposites form the basis of all plot and action. Their conflict can propel a story from beginning to end.

Think of the great antagonistic characters from literature. Sherlock Holmes had Professor Moriarty. Ripley (Sigourney Weaver) had the creature and the corporation in the film *Alien*. Remember Dr. Fu Manchu and his nemesis Denis Nayland Smith (aided by Dr. Petrie - shades of Holmes and Watson). In comic books you have Superman and Lex Luthor, Batman against the Joker and the Penguin. In *Lord of the Rings,* it was Gandalf against Sauron, and in *Star Wars,* it was Luke Skywalker and friends pitted against The Emperor and his evil factotum Darth Vader.

Your "evil bad guy" doesn't need to be human at all. It could be an alien or an artificial intelligence. Or even more sinister and unconquerable, the antagonist can be Nature, and the battle is still Good (the protagonist hero) against the Cosmos Itself which is out to destroy him. Think of Carl Stephenson's short story *Leiningen Versus the Ants* or the movie *The Perfect Storm*. In the first, the enemy is an army of all-devouring ants; in the latter, it's sea and storm. In the first, man prevails; in the second . . . well, you know how that turned out. In both, Nature was the protagonist's enemy. All the other conflicts in both stories, though between humans and with appropriate interpersonal consequences, were of secondary importance.

One final general suggestion: be clear on who performs what role in the story. A website I discovered cautions that investigators should study the "victimology" of the situation. Determine who the true victim of a crime is. Is it an individual, an insurance company, a government unit, a church, or society at large? Examine the prior history of both victims and witnesses to find people's personal issues and hidden motives.

I know this sounds like a great deal of work for you as a writer, but you want a rich fantasy life anyway, right? Create a world for yourself, people it with well thought out imaginary characters, and live in that world during your writing. If you do it well, your readers will want to visit that world with you.

Character Description

How detailed should character descriptions be? Do you have to describe every pore on a character's face? There are authors who do exactly that. Other authors might not describe a character at all, except perhaps to say that he was taller or shorter than the protagonist, or bald, or broad rather than tall. Which is the correct approach? Neither. Or both. It depends on your personal preference as the creator of your fictional world, and as dictated by the demands of your story.

My critique group regularly asks me for detailed descriptions of my characters. Some stories simply don't need it. I'm more interested in the characters' mental states than the color of their eyes. Not only that, but I'm letting my readers have a little fun by allowing them to help invent the characters for themselves. Let them envision the bravest most handsome hero or exquisitely beautiful heroine, the most vile-looking villain, the creepiest henchpersons. Let the readers inspire or terrify themselves. A radical idea? Maybe for some people. Not for me.

    To my puny male mind, "Who are you wearing?" is a ridiculous question. Personally, I don't have the vast knowledge of clothing designers, differing modes and fashions for winter or summer, types of women's shoes, and the like to make a credible detailed clothing description. More sophisticated (more acculturated?) writers might mention the designer or manufacturer of a woman's hat. Since I don't pay much attention to fashion, as my personal raiment attests, I can't do that. I let my readers do the work for me. Your readers can take part in the creation event by imagining their own character descriptions within the broad outlines that you provide. Besides, there are other ways to put flesh on a character.

    It's possible to describe a character with dialog from other characters. Don't ignore this method. Let one character notice and remark on the personal characteristics of another character: the ever-present purple plaid backpack, the constant scratching behind his left ear, the Dali-inspired waxed mustache, the rattlesnake tattoo peeking out of the perp's shirt collar. "One leg seemed to be shorter than the other, and those cold green eyes of his…"

    This technique comes in handy for description of places as well. Put the description in the mouths or minds of the characters. It no longer needs to be a "dark and stormy night." Instead, "The incessant slanting rain soaked through his thin shirt, and the cutting wind evaporated the moisture away again, driving his body temperature down towards hypothermia." A bit florid perhaps, but you get the idea.

(Author's note: The preceding short paragraph can be the key to worlds of descriptive writing. Don't let its conciseness trick you into thinking that this is an insignificant idea.)

Behavior is a descriptor, too. Think of a character who always chews gum, has a habit of rubbing his unshaven chin, limps, makes chairs creak with his weight, or has a facial tic. How about the cop in the film *Blade Runner* who leaves origami animals everywhere he goes? How unique. There's no confusing that guy with anyone else. Of course, he wasn't in Phillip K. Dick's original short story, *Do Androids Dream of Electric Sheep*, but neither was there a building named "The Bradbury." Excellent filmmaking gimmicks. Apply the same creativity in your writing.

Exercises – Character Description

- Write a dialog between two characters that details everything your readers need to know about a third character.
- List ten habits or behaviors that you haven't seen in other writer's stories, but which would provide immediate identification of your characters.
- And just for the experience, write a detailed physical description of a character. Use a character of your own invention or pick one from something you've read.

Protagonist

The protagonist is the featured character. He/she might be the hero/heroine who solves the crime and saves civilization. There might be a time when the protagonist is the villain, and the story might be told from that person's viewpoint. But in many cases, the protagonist will be the square-jawed guy in the white hat and with teeth that glint in the sunlight, or the sylphlike maiden with the oh-so-clever mind.

The story you write is the protagonist's story. It will track his/her invitation into the dilemma, pitfalls encountered, struggles to overcome obstacles, depression, failure, and ultimately resolve in either triumph or despair. This is the much spoken of "character arc." The character may change as the story progresses, and many writing gurus demand that the character does so.

Phillip Marlowe, Raymond Chandler's hard-nosed and cynical private investigator, doesn't change much except to become more cynical. Sue Grafton's character Kinsey Milhone didn't seem to change either, though the stories vary widely in their plots. She begins to evolve when her estranged family reaches out to her. Janet Evonovich's

Stephanie Plum doesn't seem to change at all, but neither do the stories. I don't think my Ben Bones character changes much either. I'm now studying how to help him grow.

Does the character have to change? I don't know. Who's to say? If your characters are engaging enough, it might not matter. Evonovich tells the same story again and again with the same characters and their unchanging personalities, and she seems to do just fine.

But there are many writing coaches who advise, nay, require, that a character evolve during the course of a story. Certainly over the life of a series. Growth is good in anyone, and it can provide many plot opportunities for future adventures.

Above all, your main characters must not be flat. They must have realistic personalities and quirks that real people might possess. No individual is all good or all bad. It's even said that Hitler loved dogs. I wonder what Stalin loved. What does your character love or hate? Does he/she belong to a political party? Why? Does he/she volunteer at the local homeless shelter, or a reading service for the blind? Why? Does he/she collect stamps, build wooden ship models, or go out occasionally dressed as the opposite sex? See what I mean? Play with it.

Exercises – Character

- Develop the back story for a featured character. Include birthplace, birthday, social class, upbringing, elementary education, talents, childhood hobbies, higher education, first and subsequent jobs, skills developed, adult hobbies, sexual orientation, personal foibles, adult height and weight, physical abnormalities, where he/she fits in the social hierarchy, friends and enemies,

etc. Write it in outline or prose form, or whatever is comfortable. Your choice.
- When you are done with this exercise, you should understand your character's habits, proclivities, and motivations. Dialogue from this character should begin to flow naturally, as do the choices he/she makes to defeat obstacles and in pursuit of his/her goals.
- Do this for each significant character. It's a sure cure for the cardboard characters we all seek to avoid.

Sidekicks

Not all protagonists need sidekicks. Some protagonists are fine on their own. Phillip Marlowe, V.I. Warshawski and Kinsey Milhone all do quite well by themselves. True, they live with recurring characters, occasionally call in a temporary helper, or use their contacts to find specific information, but for the most part, they are solos.

The sidekick can provide any number of things in your story. When we think of Sherlock Holmes, we think of the bumbling Dr. Watson as portrayed by Nigel Bruce in the films from the 1930s and 1940s. In the current Sherlock iterations, Watson (as played by Jude Law) is a rough-and-tumble man of action. Even Charlie Chan had his sons and Birmingham Brown.

Stephanie Plum is put forth as a solo who works by herself, but she is invariably accompanied by Lola, and Ranger or her cop boyfriend Joe Morelli regularly come to her aid when she's out of her depth, which is her "normal" condition.

My own serial character, Ben Bones, Consulting Genealogist and Articulator of Family Skeletons, has been working by himself and only using the skills and information provided by people he meets along the way during his adventures. Lately though, I've been thinking that he could profit from having a partner who goes on his adventures with him. It would serve to humanize him a bit, and I think it might appeal to readers. (Just thinking out loud: maybe Ben could use a secretary or home base support person or even a mentor whom he could contact with research questions and other support issues.)

Sidekicks can be male or female, brawny or scrawny, bright or dim. They are usually helpful, but not as brilliant as the protagonist. They will of course tote the luggage. They will also occasionally forget to bring the most important tool. They can provide comic relief to the story's tension by their bumbling around.

Sidekicks sometimes call attention to the all-important but unnoticed clue. Perhaps most usefully, they also act as foils to the protagonist's thinking out loud. And conveniently for the author (that would be you), they invariably ask the exact correct question at the exact correct time, which leads to the protagonist's "Aha!" realization and to the solution of the particular quandary.

Exercises – Sidekicks

- List at least five well known protagonists and their sidekicks not mentioned in this text. Identify those sidekicks' unique characteristics (if any) and define their specific roles.
- Think of five characteristics a sidekick might have. They can be physical, mental, financial or something else entirely, and they may be either positive or irritating.
- List five reasons a sidekick would become a sidekick for the heroic crime solving protagonist. What do they get out of the relationship?

Villains

In most mysteries, perhaps in all, there is usually only one primary evil doer. Even with armies composed of thousands of followers, there should be only one central character who motivates the rest of the horde. The henchmen may be bad people in themselves, but their evil is performed in the service of a master's "Grand Scheme," whether to Conquer the Known Universe, or simply to steal the day's earning from the hot dog vender on the street corner.

Why is the bad guy bad?

Just as you have to know the protagonist hero's life story to make the character live, breathe, and speak like a real human being, so you have to create a thorough back story for your villains. They must not be caricatures of themselves. If they aren't fully three dimensional, your reading audience may not stick with you until the story's end, and they will certainly not be looking forward to your next attempt.

Exercises – Villain

- Analyze your potential creep. Give five substantial reasons why a villain might be bad. These might be childhood experiences, conscious life choices, or psychological issues.
- Write a detailed biographical back story for your villain.
- Why would a villain choose a particular type of crime to perpetrate? Give four believable rationales for various criminal endeavors.

Henchmen

These people are usually secondary characters, but they need to be believable, too. As their creator, you should be aware of their needs and issues. They should have them, although not necessarily to the same degree as your primary bad guy's motivations.

Why would a person place themselves in a position of subservience and loyalty (?) to an evil genius? Or even to a small time inept crook? Money? Philosophical agreement with the boss? Were they blackmailed into being an unwilling helper? Is your henchman more or less evil than the boss? (Think of Cardinal Richelieu's henchman Count de Rochefort in Alexander Dumas' *The Three Musketeers*.) How might "plausible deniability" figure into your story?

How loyal should the henchperson be? Would he die for the master? Is he/she totally committed to the master's nefarious scheme? Why? If not, why not? What would drive a henchman to abandon his/her master? To save himself? To reward the protagonist for saving his/her life? Would a henchperson ever have a sudden change of heart? Why?

I have to apologize for the title to this

section. To be politically correct, I suppose these people should be called "henchpersons." Do I really have to give "equal opportunity" to all that overly sensitive stuff, or are we all going to act like adults with common sense?

Exercises – Henchman (Henchpersons!)

- Give five reasons why a henchman might ally himself with a bad guy leader. What might a henchman gain in the bargain?
- List several different types of "henchpersons" and the roles they might play for their boss. Note: these do not have to be "full time" henchmen.
- List five circumstances in which a henchman might abandon his/her master's scheme.

Love Interest

A love interest in a mystery can serve several useful purposes:
- Cohort or crime solving sidekick of the protagonist.
- Romance. Enhances (humanizes) the protagonist dimensionally.
- Bait, hostage, or pawn for the bad guy's nefarious deeds.
- Distraction from the true trail of clues and problem-solving.
- Relief from the tension created by the story.
- Provide a secondary story line.
- The love interest may turn out to be the villain.

The love interest can be someone the protagonist meets during his/her current case. He/she might be a help or a hindrance depending on what your story requires. They might provide help themselves, or they might call for help once, twice, or continually.

The love interest could be someone from the character's past who reappears in the present story. The character might play a part in the current dilemma, or might simply be a "ghost" or memory of a failed relationship that haunts the protagonist's thinking. The protagonist might dwell on a deceased lover, wife, or husband and be distracted from concentrating on the case as a result.

The love interest might be an artifact of an unconsummated relationship. Use simmering regret to throw your protagonist off his/her mission at critical moments when attention needs to be otherwise focused.

A love interest can be the protagonist's lingering adolescent fantasy.

The love interest might be a same sex dalliance or full-blown (did I really write that?) affair during the protagonist's "experimental" teen period.

A love interest might be fiercely loyal or a back-stabbing double-crosser. They come in all flavors, just like real people.

The love interest can be hetero or gay, just as the protagonist might be. A gay protagonist or a former same sex lover might develop an often ignored readership into a solid fan base. Not that we writers are that calculating and manipulative of our audience, but think about it.

Exercises – Love Interest

- List five positive qualities for a love interest. How might they help your story?
- List five negative or potentially problematic qualities for a love interest. How might they complicate things for your protagonist?
- Sketch out a short scenario showing how the protagonist's love interest might create problems in the story.

Cops

The police figure strongly in many of our stories. A police character might even serve as your protagonist.

Think of the advantages a cop character brings to a story: professional training, learning gained from a great deal of direct on-the-job experience, departmental resources, professional contacts in and out of the policeman's law enforcement world, knowledge of the local underworld, consultation with colleagues, an expense account and/or a budget. In general, a policeman is a lay psychologist, is professionally skeptical and suspicious, is intelligent, observant, competent, and determined (dogged). Wow! I just impressed myself with that list. Now that I'm thinking about it, a cop would make a great protagonist.

Your police character doesn't have to be the cop on the beat or the lead detective in an investigation. Think of other roles that police officials play. How about the police commissioner, the forensics people, the dispatcher who takes the call that starts the story? A cop might be a victim, or might even turn out to be the perpetrator.

And let's not forget about the disgraced or discredited former cop. Why was this cop fired or asked to resign from the force? Perhaps it was to save embarrassment for higher-ups. How big is the bag of sour grapes this character lugs around? What did this character learn from that experience? Is he/she still the same irritating windbag that got fired, or has there been a mellowing over time? How about the people who remained behind with the department? Are they still up to the same old tricks?

Exercises – Police

- Sign up for your local Citizens Police Academy. Many cities and counties offer this intensive learning opportunity. You will gain many insights into police organization and procedure that will enrich your writing.
- Check with your local police force to see if they have a "ride-along" program. Learn how your local gendarmes work the community by actually seeing them in action. (I was astonished to hear that my local police force would let me carry a licensed firearm on my ride-along. It was left up to the officer I would be riding with whether to allow it or not. He didn't, by the way, which I thought was sensible.) Be sure to thank your police "tour guide" when the ride is over.
- List five different roles an official police character might play in your story.

Minor Characters for Color

These are the spear carriers, the witnesses who see the same or differing events and whose stories don't match, the corner drug dealer, the cab drivers who can provide information on pickup points and destinations, the bartenders who "Never heard of him," or who grew up with him and know the guy's whole life history.

These folks can provide all the background, place, and character description you need. In fact, I'm now thinking of writing a story told completely by these "little people," by the background characters. There might even be no protagonist at all. An interesting challenge, don't you think?

Point of View (POV)

General Considerations

Humans can be too analytical sometimes, and I think that people make the subject of POV too complex. Keep it simple. It's easier to see through the fog. The basic principles are:

- Who is telling the story?
- Whose story is it?
- What do they know?
- At what point do they learn what they know?

You have several traditional choices. They are first person, third person, or omniscient narrator (god mode).

An English grammar book will also talk about second person, but for the mystery writer, second person isn't a good choice. If I were giving you orders or detailing how to assemble the latest gizzywhomper you just bought, I would talk to you in 2nd person. "Place Tab A into Slot B." For story telling, it doesn't work.

One of the worst things you can do as a writer, something that will confuse and probably irritate your readers, is called "head-hopping." Simply stated, this means switching viewpoints within paragraphs or chapters. If you plan on telling the story through various characters at different times, be sure it's clear which character is telling the story at any point.

First Person

First person narration means that the person the story happened to, the person who had the adventure, is doing the talking. He/she can tell the story as it's happening, or as a report of what happened in the past.

A benefit of first person narration is the immediacy of the tale. The first person speaker, many times the protagonist, also has built-in veracity because he/she has had the experience.

The problem with a first person narrator is that the teller doesn't always know everything that's happening as it happens. He generally knows everything by the end of the story, just like the reader, but he often arrives at this state of total knowledge after the reader has. That's okay most of the time, and it can be used to build surprises into the story. For example, the protagonist narrator's motorcycle is racing toward the one lane bridge that the bad guy has blown up, but the hero won't know it until he's gone over the precipice at 70 miles per hour. If the entire story is in first person, the reader won't know about the destroyed bridge either. Surprise!

Sue Grafton's PI Kinsey Milhone is an interesting example, since these stories, though seeming to be told as they happen, occasionally end with her signature, *Respectfully submitted*, at the end of a report. The ancient radio show *Yours Truly, Johnny Dollar* ("The transcribed adventures of the man with the action-packed expense account — America's fabulous freelance insurance investigator") ended its stories the same way. It remains a workable format.

First person viewpoint may also be used by someone who is reporting on what happened after the fact when the case has been closed. A cohort can be the best teller of the story. Think about Dr. John Watson, Sherlock Holmes' companion and chronicler, as a prime example of this character role. This method provides a first person point of view and simultaneously prevents the main character from sounding like a pompous braggart who is always promoting himself.

I like to write from the first person perspective. I feel comfortable in this voice. It provides plenty of opportunity for me to rant about things and thinly disguise it as the character's internal monologue.

Third Person - Omniscient Narrator or God Mode

Looking down from my perch high up on Mount Olympus, I can easily observe the doings of all the mortals below. They cannot hide from me. I can tell you what each of them is doing at any time, whether they can see one another or not.

In omniscient mode, the narrator knows everything about anything that's happening everywhere at all times, even though the characters might not know. It's your decision as author how much your story teller will reveal to the reader, and when.

In the motorcycle and bridge example, the motorcycle rider will be ignorant of the danger, but you as omniscient author may have already informed the reader of what's coming. This will create tension and suspense for the reader. If the reader has seen the villain booby trap or destroy the bridge, he/she can be terrified for the cyclist, but can't stop it from happening. The cyclist won't know about it until it's too late. Too bad for him.

Exercises – POV

- Write a paragraph from a first person perspective. Keep the action simple.
Example: "From the bow of the ship, I watched the disaster as it happened."
- Rewrite the paragraph using a third person perspective. Compare the two. Do they both work? Which do you prefer?
Example: "John saw it all from his post at the bow of the ship. He watched as the disaster was unfolding, unable to help."

Plotting and Scheming

Thinking Inside Out

When beginning a journey, it always helps to know where you're starting from, as well as where you're going, even if you don't know the exact route you'll take.

You have the same vital concerns in story telling. Where does the story begin? And where is it supposed to end up? These are opposite poles of your story.

Start with these questions when building a plot, but here's the trick to it: the answer isn't directly linear. Even if you know the story's central dilemma, the "why" of the story, you should try to think from your plot's destination backwards to your starting point.

With knowledge of the story's resolution, you can figure out what clues need to be uncovered along the way, and at what point they must emerge from the background noise. You can decide what ancillary characters need to appear, and when they must disappear, when and where the death weapon will be discovered, and who needs to die and when.

Different writers approach a story in different ways. Some have a definite end that they feel they must reach. They might build their story backwards as I've suggested. Others might write from the beginning without a plan, letting the story play itself out as determined by the characters' natural actions until a first rough draft is written. They will then go back and start again through the story, restructuring chapters and scenes, and placing clues and red herrings in appropriate places. Other writers might think everything through and outline scene by scene in great detail, then fleshing out the skeleton with full text.

It's up to you which method you will be most comfortable with. Experiment. I've done it all these different ways, as well as synthesizing from pieces of the various methods. Let the story determine the way it wants (needs?) to be developed and written. Don't force it.

I have a good spatial conceptual brain. On an IQ test for example, if you show me a picture of a flattened out three dimensional object, I can invariably match it with a picture of the assembled object. But when I began woodworking, I couldn't for the life of me figure out what parts a bookcase had to have to make it into a physical reality. I could see the completed bookcase in my mind, and I could draw an isometric image of it. But to think inside out, to unravel the structure from the finished product, to define and design all the individual pieces, and figure out in which order to cut and assemble them . . . I can't do it. Everyone has their limitations. That's one of mine.

But I can build a story. I can see the linearity in reverse from the end of the perp's career back to its start. I can think through a timeline and place events along it to tell the tale.

That's what you have to do, even though you might not have a resolution in mind when you begin. You might only have a dilemma to confront your protagonist with. That's all right. Throw him into the maelstrom, then let him find his own way to safety. He will, unless you're determined to kill him off altogether.

The first rough draft is supposed to be a raw and ragged gush of ideas. Don't despair. It's only a starting point. During your rewrite(s), you'll be changing the plot flow and weaving in all those red herrings that keep your readers guessing, and inserting the clues that help them solve the puzzle. Your characters might even come to a completely different resolution than you first envisioned. After all, it's their story, right? Let them figure it out. You're only the writer. It's your job to watch the movie in your imagination and translate the characters' actions into words so that a reader can follow what's happening.

The Dreaded Outline

To outline or not to outline: that is the question (with my most sincere apologies to William S.).

The controversy over the question of outlining, of planning a story or novel out from the beginning to the end, has plagued writers since quill was first put to paper. I don't doubt that more than one bloody nose has been produced in the course of the discussion.

An outline is a road map. It tells you where you start, and it takes you along with supreme confidence right to the end. In my humble opinion, an outline can be very helpful.

Having said that, let me also say that at the time of this writing, there are two novels sitting uncompleted in my computer, and I blame the highly detailed step by step outlines that I spent so many hours building before I started writing the text. Because I nailed everything down so thoroughly, where the characters were when this or that happened, when the clues appeared, the venues in which things happened, and their order of happening, my outline became a quicksand of my own making. I'm trapped in the concrete I poured around my imagination's ankles. I believe this.

It's going to be tough for me to let go of those outlines. I've had such faith in them for so long. But let go I must, or those two books will never be completed and find their way out into the world to make me rich and famous.

There are writers who say they never outline. These are the "pantsers," the "seat-of-the-pants" type writers who sit down at their word processors and just let it flow. Some of them are very successful artistically and commercially. For the longest time I didn't know how they could do it. It seemed altogether too disorganized, but somehow it worked for them.

Did you ever hear of NaNoWriMo? That's the National Novel Writing Month. It's an online challenge to write 50,000 words within the 30 days of the NaNoWriMo month of November, without a previously worked out plan. If you write 1,667 words per day, you'll at least make it to a rough first draft.

I heard about this craziness two days before the end of October 2012 and decided to try it. I went online to www.nanowrimo.org and signed up. Not knowing what to write about, I suspended my other writing projects and twenty-four days later, I had a pretty good story of 32,444 words. Did it matter that I didn't reach 50k? Not to me. Here's what I accomplished:

- I had faced a serious writing challenge, complete with a deadline.
- I ended up with a great little mystery story, *The Extra Body*.
- I had gotten into the habit of writing every morning when I got up, and most days almost reaching the recommended 1,667 words per day. This in itself was a great accomplishment, and served to overcome my lazy procrastinating bum writing habits.
- I had actually written a story with no pre-planning. This was a major first for me, and a huge psychological hurdle for this over-planner. I felt I could now return with a new flexibility to my two

novel projects that had become mired by over-planning.
- I created characters who acted on their own and essentially told me what to type. I recorded it all as I sat and watched the movie play out in my head.
- By the end, I felt like a writer, with new confidence in my ability to write and in my creative capacity.

I can now recommend NaNoWriMo to any writers who need a push from outside to get going, or to anyone stuck in a writing quagmire. NaNoWriMo can shake you loose. The challenge and the experience were invaluable for me.

So what's the right answer: to outline or not to outline? I think the answer is somewhere in between the absolutes, as with so many things in life. If you can produce credible and saleable work without any planning, more power to you. I couldn't. But I now know that I can loosen up from the rigidity of my outlines, to be a more flexible writer and find a middle ground between chaos and military precision. Don't expect me to give you a hard rule on this point. There isn't one.

In the end, you'll have to find your own answer. No one method is right for everyone. You'll have to experiment. Sometimes you'll fail, but sometimes you'll succeed. How and why is up to you. As for myself, I have my own problems to solve, my own answers to find. And the struggle begins anew with each writing project.

Outlining for Analysis

Many of us learn by copying other people's work. That's fine, but be careful of plagiarism. There's much to be learned from studying the work of other writers. Maybe you won't do an outline for your own work, but I recommend outlining someone else's.

You might do what I did once when I was thinking about writing a romance novel. I bought half a dozen of them at my local used paperback store and tore through them in a couple of hours looking for how it was done. I never did write the thing, but it was a quickie course that only cost me a couple of bucks. I learned a bunch about character, story structure, and plot.

Exercises – Analysis

- Pick a writer whose work you like. Dashiell Hammett or Raymond Chandler are good people to start with. A Robert D. Parker Spenser novel would be good, too. Take the books apart by reading them with a critical eye. Don't just read the books without taking notes. Write your observations down and look them over later. For each book, note the following:
- How is the story structured?
- Where does the story begin?
- How many story lines are there? What are they?
- When do the characters appear? Do they appear fully fleshed out, or is the true character revealed a bit at a time?
- List the clues, both "real" and red herrings? When do they appear? How are they introduced?
- Diagram the "story arc." Show the flow of the story from intro, through crises and their resolutions, all the way to the ending. See how the author built

tension?

Who Done It?

Do you need to know this when you start your project? Some writers adamantly say yes, but others, equally adamant, say no.

For me, fiction writing is an organic process. I've worked knowing my villain from the start and not knowing, and have completed books and short stories either way. If you're writing factual material, a textbook on weather for example, by all means outline from beginning to end before starting to write. It's not only safer, but you can sell the book on a proposal and detailed outline before you start creating the body text itself.

But fiction is a different kind of creature. As you write, situations change, characters grow, plot elements arise that weren't envisioned in the beginning. This is natural. Don't get upset about these developments. Take advantage of the good ideas and throw away the others. Perhaps you can even use the rejects in your next piece. Let the characters act out the story's resolution themselves. Trust me; all will be revealed in the end, to you as well as to your readers.

Of course, if you have a first class villain character who simply demands to do the nasty deeds, follow that plan. If an arch villain like the whacky scientist Romero in the film *Spy Kids2: The Island of Lost Dreams* propels your plot, there might be no way to avoid him.

But after my 2012 NaNoWriMo writing experience, I can say that you don't have to know at the start whether the butler did it, or if it was Mrs. Mockingbird in the billiard room with the rolling pin. In fact, even if you think you know who done did it at the start, you might be surprised as the plot twists and turns and the planned perp turns into a red herring and a totally different character ends up being a more logical villain for the piece.

Whatever you do, don't try to force the plot. Just because you want X to be the perp, don't will it to happen. Your writing will feel like that's exactly what you did.

The Opening Situation

Where will your reader meet your protagonist? And what condition will the character be in when met? Will he/she be in great danger, perhaps hanging off a cliff while grasping a loosely rooted clump of weeds? Think of the books that held your interest from the very first sentence. That's what you want to do to your readers, too.

You generally want your readers to meet your lead character and see the character's problem from the start. You want to give your reader a reason to root for the character.

It's good to hit your reader with an action sequence right away. Murder your first victim in the opening sentences. Find the first corpse at the very start, or at least discover evidence that a murder, diamond theft, or embezzlement (insert your preferred crime here) has occurred. Start pointing fingers at potential perpetrators.

A word about prologues. Several of my Ben

Bones genealogical mysteries begin with a prologue. Why is this? Although the story happens and is solved in the present, the issues are generated in historical events. Thus, I feel obligated to set the stage for the story and establish a background for my readers before actually launching into Ben's contemporary adventure.

Sometimes the prologue is a historical setting that sets the game into motion. Once it was a leap to a crisis in the middle of the story, after which the story backed up to the beginning and ran to catch up with that crisis.

Some members of my critique group object to my prologues. They consider them to be tedious info dumps and feel that a prologue postpones hooking my readers, perhaps until it's too late.

So what's the answer? As usual, there isn't one answer that's true for all writers in all situations. In the immortal words of Mr. Natural (from *R.Crumb Comics*), "Use the right tool for the job." Build your prologue to suit your story. Some stories will demand a prologue; others will not. Maybe you can silence your critics by calling your prologue "Chapter One," and going on from there. Let the demands of better storytelling decide what you do.

The Hook

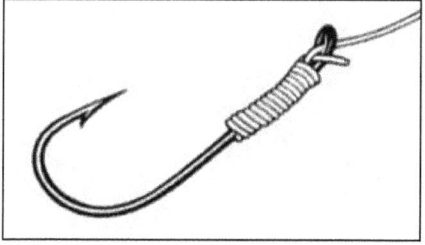

The specific language used to open your story is a critical consideration. The opening paragraph, and many would say the very first sentence, is where you are going to capture your reader and make him want to read the next sentence, the next paragraph, the next chapter, and so on to the resolution of the protagonist's dilemma. With today's audiences and the typically short attention spans they have, if you don't catch your readers at the very start, they may wander off looking for another book to read.

The hook is different from the opening situation. The situation may show the protagonist in mortal danger or the world about to be devoured by aliens, but a great situation can be defused by bland writing.

The hook must be exciting and should startle your reader. It must express the situation in an uncommon way, perhaps with a twist of viewpoint or by drawing a contradictory conclusion from facts that point in a different direction than the obvious. Present the facts in a novel way. The opening paragraph can grab your reader's attention or chase him away.

Exercises – The Hook

- Write an opening sentence for your current project which will grab a reader's attention and not let the reader escape.
  Example: As the blazing building's structure began to fail around me, I knew my love for her would kill me this time.
- Write another hook from a different angle.
  Example: She watched the blazing building collapse and knew she had finished him off at last after so many attempts.

Foreshadowing

Foreshadowing is simply inserting clues related to what's coming in the future.

Foreshadowing is for the reader, but not necessarily for the characters.

How much foreshadowing is enough? How much is too much? Like any sharp instrument, it depends on the skill with which it's wielded that makes all the difference. You don't want to give the plot away to your readers too early in the story. What you want to do is give a hint of what's to come without giving the story away completely or losing the reader's interest.

You might place a prop in an early chapter that the reader remembers later when it's finally used. You might show the villain in the library reading a forensic text on exotic poisons. Will a poison be used later? Maybe. Or it might be a red herring clue. The villain might later decide that poison is too subtle and that his crime requires a bomb instead.

Foreshadowing is the great "cliff hanger" chapter ending. It's a writer's gimmick that forces the reader to continue reading instead of putting the book down for the day. He's simply got to find out what's going to happen next. Is this manipulating the reader? Of course it is. But feel no guilt. If done well, it will win fans for your "I couldn't stop reading" writing. An enthused fan will go out searching for the next adventure in the series. He/She might even tell his/her friends about the great characters recently discovered. And that's the goal, isn't it?

Foreshadowing might be an afterthought for the author, requiring you to go through the text from the beginning seeding clues here and there because of what happens later in the story. The story will tell you what it needs and when, if you pay close attention.

Internal Continuity

Unless you're writing a group of disconnected short pieces, the internal consistency of your story is critical. If your villain is left-handed in the first chapter, she'd better still be left-handed when she's finished off in chapter 56. If the murder weapon we see fired in the opening scene is a .38 caliber Smith & Wesson Model 10 with a 3-inch barrel, the murder gun found at the end by your heroic and brilliant detective can't be a .32 caliber Smith & Wesson Model 10 with a 6-inch barrel.

Sounds simple? Well, it's not. It demands strict attention to detail, and on a continuing basis. Motion picture companies hire people to watch for these kinds of errors when filming. It's amateurish and doesn't work if the blue lampshade is suddenly a polka dot shade in the same room in a later scene. In movies, the left-handed, right-handed error is tricky to catch. The classic anachronistic gaffe is the Timex wristwatch on a medieval soldier.

If you're writing a series, be sure the back story on your characters doesn't change from book to book. I made this mistake myself. My series character Ben Bones was supposed to marry a particular lady doctor in the first book, but in the second book, the back story says he'd married a childhood sweetheart. Oops. That cost me hours of anguished writing to correct the error, and several hundred dollars for a second print run. The defective books are on a shelf waiting for a featured role in next winter's fireplace.

Eye color doesn't change, unless colored contact lenses are used as part of a character's disguise. Height doesn't change, unless height adjusters are purposely used inside a character's shoes. Hair color can be changed with bleach or dye. But these are all superficial attributes. The basic character must be consistent throughout.

Story Structure, Logic, & Time

How do you get from the beginning of the story to the end? Will it make sense? Or are you forcing the ending that you had in mind when you began in spite of the way the story wants to be told?

A story must have an internal logic. Unless you're writing a free-flowing fantasy tale, it must make sense. Fact *A* does not necessarily have to lead the reader directly to conclusion *B*, but the story has to get there sooner or later.

The Story Arc

Ask anyone with a degree in English Lit or Creative Writing and they're bound to launch into a discussion of the much cited Story Arc. If you'd asked me about it two years ago, I would've said I don't know what you're talking about. I don't have either one of those degrees.

But being an autodidact, I've gone and done some reading about the concept, and I might have a basic understanding of it... at least enough to explain it to someone who has no idea at all.

The Story Arc is also known as the Narrative Arc and, in more academic circles, the Hero's Journey. I recommend doing your own research on all three labels for greater insight. You'll then be able to synthesize your own approach. If you do a Google search for "story arc" and look at the images, you'll get a wonderful graphic view of the variety of arcs that people have come up with. Might even have a laugh or two.

It's become almost a tradition, though not a "rule," that a story is divided into three parts, like Gaul was. It's a convenient way to divide up an empire, including an empire of the mind such as your story.

The first section states the problem or dilemma. Characters good and evil can be developed here and set into motion. The tone of your story can be established.

The second section drives the characters to and through a crisis or two. In "The Hero's Journey" formula, the hero crosses from the Ordinary World into the Special World, is tested, finds allies, confronts his demons and prevails. Is all this necessary in your story? Maybe not, but it's something to think about it anyway.

The third section resolves the situation one way or another. Maybe the good guys will triumph and save the world. Maybe not. The story will let you know, if you're paying attention.

Is three the magic number for sections of a story? Not at all. The story will tell you how many sections it needs, how many crises and how many obstacles need to be overcome to reach a logical conclusion.

A Variety of Choices

How should you tell the story? There are varying modes. Some stories want to be told one way, while others demand an alternative approach. There have been instances when I've gotten to the end and discovered that the story didn't work the way I thought it would. I needed to completely restructure it into a different logical structure. This might have been a huge problem for people like Robert Lewis Stevenson and Charles Dickens writing on foolscap with quills, but thanks to computers and sophisticated word processing programs, it's a matter of cut-and-paste, after you figured out the problem and its logical solution, of course. When they work, computers are great.

Linear Mode

The most straight-forward approach is to tell your story from the beginning right through to the end in a series of incidents. These incidents require decisions and acts by your characters and will have positive or negative consequences, which the characters then have to deal with in turn.

The story might be told in omniscient mode, or it might flit from one character POV to another, but generally tending in a direct line from opening dilemma to final resolution.

Flashback Mode

Somewhere in the flow of your story, it might make sense to take the reader backward in time. Insert a flashback.

This might be done to show the placing of a clue that appears later, such as the perpetrator inadvertently dropping something at a crime scene that clearly identifies him/her. This is a great way to insert red herrings, too. Or you might want to show background interaction that determines a relationship between two characters in the story's present.

The trick with flashbacks is not to confuse the reader. I've seen authors title a flashback with a date and time. If other chapters are titled similarly, there's no problem.

Flash-forward Mode

The flash-forward can occur at any point in your narrative. It might appear at the beginning of the narrative, or it might need to show up later, but before the very end. There might be several in a book. Where it appears is up to you the writer as you follow the demands of the story's logic.

I began one Ben Bones adventure with a flash-forward prologue to a crisis that occurred about a third of the way through the story. The formal first chapter which followed went back in time to the beginning, continuing on until the story had caught up with the prologue event. Did it work? I believe it did. Other people think it did.

Reverse Mode

Start at the end of the story and work your way backwards in time toward the point where the protagonist first becomes involved, perhaps by finding the first corpse or clue. I haven't tried this yet, but the idea intrigues.

The Chapter

Traditionally, the chapter provides logical breaks in the storytelling. It's a way to organize events spatially, temporally, emotionally, or by character.

Spatially, you might group all the events that happen in Location A in one chapter, then go on to Location B in the next chapter, and so on, returning to previous locations as required by the story.

Temporally, chapters may follow one another in the order that events occur. You might mix them up a bit, but be careful about confusing your readers. This technique might work if you are presenting differing stories witnesses tell about the same event. You would necessarily return to the same starting point for each witness. Remember Kurosawa's 1950 film *Roshamon?* That's exactly what he did, character by character.

Chapters may have one or more scenes in them, which brings us to the next topic.

The Scene

The scene is the basic building block of your story. Action and interaction happen within scenes.

How does one define a piece of a piece? It's not a fragment because it might be complete within itself. Or it might seem complete, but without more, it may have little significance.

Perhaps I can analogize by using the structure of the human body.

Assume the entire body to be the entire story, the book. The head, arms, legs and other discrete sections can represent chapters. And within each chapter, the hand as example, each individual bone corresponds to a scene. Together, several scenes comprise a chapter. The chapters, all together, comprise the entire story. That's as far as this tortured analogy can go.

This all became clearer to me when I began using yWriter (available free from the website http://www.spacejock.com/yWriter5.html) to organize one of my writing projects. Besides being able to list individual characters and their characteristics, specific items in use and when and where they appear, and event locations, the program's handling of chapters and the scenes within them was enlightening. I'm told that Scrivener can provide authors the same sort of detail and overview.

Moving the Story Forward

The loss of a story's momentum can be fatal,

and a story without forward motion can lose the reader.

If the story pauses while you fill in historical background or grind through lengthy and beautifully crafted descriptive passages, you're in danger of losing readers. Readers these days don't have the patience for it. Television, films and commercials have conditioned them; they want to see the next explosion.

That's not to say that you need an explosion, car chase, or fist fight in every scene. That would be too much. But it's important for the story to keep going and not stall on the tracks.

How is it done? It's simple. Think of your story as a drunk stumbling home from a night out at the neighborhood pub. He puts one foot forward and falls toward it, then falls forward onto the next extended foot... all the way home. Just as the drunk uses his forward momentum to make progress, your story must also tumble forward toward solution, and seem to do so without effort.

One method to accomplish this is clever and skillful foreshadowing. The final sentence of a scene or chapter should give a hint, a hook, or cliffhanger that will cause the reader to want to know what happens next. Will the motorcyclist hero drive off the destroyed bridge into oblivion? Will the stalled airplane crash into the mountain killing all onboard and ending your story right there? Will the hero break a tooth on the diamond in the pastrami sandwich he's about to bite into? Get the idea?

Pacing

Pacing is not the speed at which things happen. It's the rhythm.

If your characters are racing from one location to the next, if the bombs keep falling and there's never a chance for you, your characters, or your readers to pause and take a deep breath, that's no good. There has to be a break in the action sometimes, perhaps after a danger had been defeated, an obstacle overcome, or a bomb defused, that eases the tension until the next crisis.

Think of a roller coaster. It doesn't always climb slowly nor rush its descent precipitously. The slow climbs serve to build tension that is ultimately released by the screaming descents.

It's the same with your story. There need to be peaks and valleys in your action, and thus in the tension the reader experiences.

The following chart shows how the action, the various crises, rise and fall, building and relieving tension through your story. Consider this an example of a narrative arc.

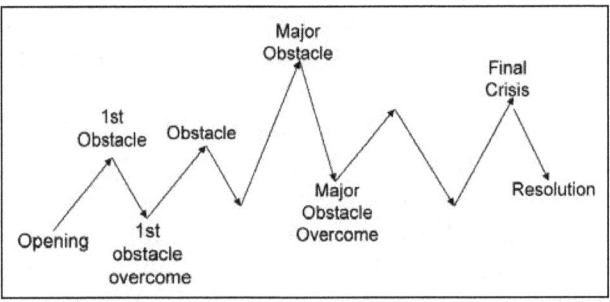

It's great to keep your readers on the edge of their seats, but give them a break once in a while.

Dialogue

Let the Characters Speak for Themselves

If you have read other books about writing fiction, you have undoubtedly come across strange statements saying that the characters have come alive and done things that the author never expected. Sounds pretty metaphysical, doesn't it? I thought so too, until it happened to me.

My character was in a tough situation. It was confrontation time, and what came out of the character's mouth totally surprised me. It wasn't at all what I'd expected. But it was the natural thing for that character to say. It was what a real character in a real situation would say and not the contrived verbiage I'd had in mind beforehand.

Not only was I surprised by his words, but it created a plot wrinkle I hadn't expected as well, one that turned out quite nicely in the larger context of the book.

If you have successfully created characters with full back stories, characters who have had lives before getting swept up in your story, they will have developed attitudes and opinions from their life experiences. They will have dealt with other situations and they will have attained a "maturity" of sorts, even if it's all imaginary. They will deal with situations as themselves, not as spokespeople for your ideas and opinions.

Let it happen. Let the characters be themselves. Let them speak for themselves and act in ways that are natural for them given their upbringing, education, and life experiences. Let their back stories grow as they live their lives in your tale.

Setting

Setting is the time, place, and conditions within which context your story happens. Setting isn't merely the locked room in which the corpse is found. Setting is several different things simultaneously, and can include:
- The environment where the action occurs, including but not limited to the room, the building, the city or town, the state and country, the micro and macro geography.
- The time period in which the action takes place, whether past, present, or

future.
- The prevailing cultural attitudes, local traditions, or myths of the time.
- The personal attitudes, philosophical stances, and psychological conditions of your characters.
- The weather. Is it the same all the time or does your story happen during an extreme weather event? Remember Edward G. Robinson, Humphrey Bogart and Lauren Bacall in the 1948 classic film *Key Largo?* The hurricane was a main character.
- The season of the year.
- Anything else that influences the who, what, where, when, why or how of your story.

For me, one of the great examples of setting to establish characters and their relationship is in Raymond Chandler's *The Big Sleep*. Remember the opening chapters in which Philip Marlowe goes to the Sternwood mansion, the description of the entry hall as being two stories high and the stained-glass panel showing a knight rescuing a lady? The tile-paved staircase, the "big, empty fireplace," the large oil portrait and cavalry pennants above the mantel? All this, and more, gives the feeling of opulence and old money. Then Lauren Bacall, excuse me, Miss Carmen Sternwood appears and tries to trip Marlowe up with her "cute" little girl seductiveness.

Marlowe meets General Sternwood in his greenhouse, in which the hot air is described as viscous and almost soggy, and filled with the "cloying smell of orchids." The glass walls dripped "big drops of moisture" everywhere. The light is described as an unreal green color. What a sensory rich description.

After making his way through this jungle environment, Marlowe finds The General seated in his wheelchair, and in that unreal scene, the characters of Marlowe, General Sternwood, and his errant daughter set, partially due to their behavior, and partly due to their milieu.

Research on setting is all important. In the past, this might have meant a tax deductible trip to the place your story is set, the purchase of maps and guidebooks, many trips to various libraries, and lots and lots of copying so you could bring your research home for later perusal. No longer.

The Internet now serves the same purpose as those red eye airline flights or extended drives. It's no longer necessary to scale the heights of your setting's mountains, to get lost in its forests, or dive to the depths of its oceans. Consider yourself liberated from the drudgery (read: fun) of distant research junkets. You are now free to stay at home, close to your refrigerator and liquor cabinet, and turn yourself into a couch potato of the classic variety while cranking out pounds and pounds of deathless prose on your laptop. The writer's world has changed.

But having the Internet handy is no excuse to neglect mapping your action. Floor plans of murder scenes, party venues, hotels and streets will help you visualize the action and keeps you consistent. They don't have to be anything fancy. Here's an example, a hotel floor plan I drew for use in writing *Ben Bones and the Conventional Murders:*

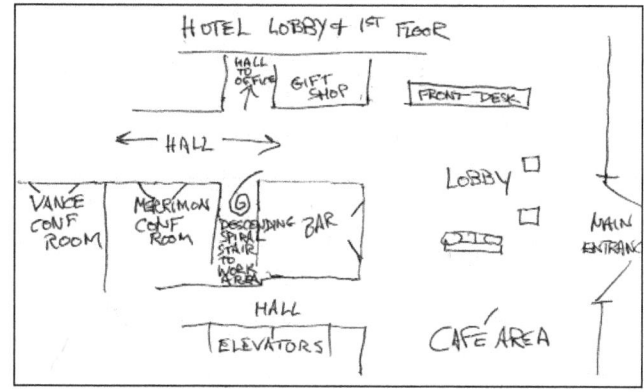

Setting doesn't have to be spelled out in all its grim detail. Dialogue can be used to show 1) that characters are aware of their environment, and 2) to inform the reader about place and its condition. Consider the following:

"It was a dark and stormy night . . ."

As opposed to:

"The trek through the woods with no moon had worn John out. The storm had soaked him to the skin and he was sore all over from the wind-whipped branches."

More words, if you measure success in word count, but the scene has also been set without a clichéd expression or an info dump.

Exercises – Setting

- In three paragraphs, describe an outdoor setting you know well: first on a summer day, then during a midwinter storm, and finally, on a moonlit night.
- In two paragraphs, describe your living room. Give all pertinent shape and content details. You may see things you never noticed before.
- Sketch a map of the area in which your story takes place. This might be several

city blocks, a country home's drawing room, the basement or treatment rooms at The Institute, or a pastoral landscape.
- Draw a floor plan of the room where the murder (or whatever crime) occurs. Where are your characters before the event, during, and after? Don't forget to draw a classic chalk line silhouette to show where the body was found.

The Sensory Environment

Let's not forget that our characters, imaginary though they are, have the same five senses that we writers have. They can see, hear, smell, touch, taste just as real human beings can, unless they're disabled in some way. Letting them experience their sensory environment will enrich your writing and the reader's pleasure.

What color was the sky at the time of the crime? The leaves on the autumn trees? The eyes of the love interest?

Did your protagonist really hear someone around the back of the house, or was it his/her imagination? Was someone whispering in the dark, or was it the wind blowing through the bare tree limbs outside the broken window?

What was the smell in the old house when your protagonist investigator first entered? Was that a clue that something was wrong? Did the smell of gasoline linger after the fire? Whether it did or not might provide a clue. What was that aroma from the suspect's clothes? Where had the protagonist encountered it before?

There was something odd about the texture under the protagonist's fingers. What felt wrong? Was it important? Or was it merely a distraction, a red herring?

Certain poisons have a distinctive taste. It might not matter with a fast acting poison, except to allow the victim a second or two of terror as the inevitable took over. How about a poison that was administered over a protracted time? Could the prospective victim detect something amiss with their evening milkshakes and point an accusing finger?

Exercises – Sensory Environment

- Describe the sound of a window being jimmied open.
- Describe a smell from your childhood. What would trigger you to remember that smell? What memories does the aroma trigger?
- Describe the feel of a burlap bag, a silk purse, a sow's ear. Consider size, shape, and texture.
- What does a mango taste like? Describe it.
- You have been given a banana split. Describe your sensations as you consume it.

Clues and Anti-clues

Be Honest With Your Readers

I saw an episode of one of my favorite television crime shows in which the good guy characters were being run crazy by some psycho killer through most of the show's hour length. No matter what they tried, they couldn't put the meager clues together to figure out who was doing it to them. The situation was getting desperate. Suddenly, in the final two minutes, a totally new character appeared from nowhere and was revealed as the perp. Case solved.

Don't EVER do that to your readers! That's a plot device called *deus ex machina* ("god from the machine"), and it's simply the cheapest of shots a desperate author can take. The situation was solved by the gods, not by your characters or the application of their skill and logic. Your readers will be let down with a bang. This same show did that in another episode several months later and took another hit to their popularity. I hope they fired those writers who had been responsible and hired real writers who could get from the beginning of a story to the end in good mental order without calling for divine intervention.

There may be times when you reach the end of the story and discover that a vital clue was never placed for the investigator to find. Figure out where it has to surface and go "seed" it there. There might be a bunch of them to fix. A word of warning: don't overdo it.

How many clues are too many? I think there should be barely enough to solve the crime or lead to the perp, but we shouldn't be tripping over them in every other scene.

How Red Should a Herring Be?

First of all, what is meant by the phrase "red herring?"

When fox hunting on horseback with packs of baying hounds was all the rage in Merry Olde England, a red (cured and salted) herring (or other stinking carcass) was dragged over the ground by servants before the event to lay a false trail for the dogs. Ah, that's it: a false trail.

In a mystery, as in politics, a red herring is a spurious element which deflects discussion away from the important point under examination.

For us as mystery writers, a red herring might be:

- A clue discovered or a comment made which seems important at the time but later proves to be insignificant or misleading.
- A clue that leads the investigator off in a wrong direction.
- A clue which identifies an innocent "guilty" party.
- Additional suspects brought into the story merely to confuse the issue for readers and the investigator.

In my humble opinion, a herring should be red enough to see when looking backwards, but not clearly an obvious false clue at the moment it's first shown to the reader. Keep your readers guessing and they'll be back for more.

Self-discipline

No matter what else is happening in your life, you have to put in your "chair time." If you don't allocate writing time for yourself and force yourself into the chair (!), the work will never be completed.

I have serious problems with this myself. I blame it on aging, reduction of available energy, and that my "productive time" is limited to the first 2-3 hours of the day. Besides all that, I'm a lazy S.O.B. Are those simply transparent excuses to go watch another Basil Rathbone *Sherlock Holmes* episode because I can't think of anything to write? I've been diagnosed as an underachiever, as ADHD, as a lazy bum, and several other things I won't mention in these pages. But I have always considered myself a driven person, and I've accomplished much creative work during my lifetime. Who's to say?

I have always had a defined place to work. A studio, a formal office, a writing room – call it what you will. It's a place where I can leave my work out and open to where I last suspended operations, so getting back to it the next day is easy. You may not have the luxury, particularly if you're a "normal" type of person with kids, a significant other, or if you're living in your parents' basement. Don't let obstacles be an excuse. Your laptop computer with multiple windows open simultaneously might be all the formal work space you need. I generally have six or seven windows open at once, and I continuously switch back and forth between the document I'm working on, several research websites, *dictionary.com* and *thesaurus.com*, and my word count spreadsheet. I don't consider this multi-tasking because I'm doing only a single thing at any time, but I'm switching around between multiple resources to do it. It's the method I've worked out for myself, but someone watching me write might become dizzy from the experience.

After the Writing

The Problem: Getting It Right

Okay, you've somehow slogged your way through the story from beginning to end. Finally, after suffering all the agonies of birthing a creative work, you have a book, sort of.

But with the feeling of completion comes a feeling of dread. Suppose your basic facts are wrong? Suppose your characters were born in years that make it impossible for them to ever exist in the same time frame? Suppose you jump tenses from sentence to sentence? Suppose your dialogue is stilted? Suppose the left-handed villain at the beginning of the book is right-handed at the end? Oops!

There are so many potential errors,

especially for new writers. What can you do to improve your product?

An often quoted writing aphorism states that it's not the writing that makes a successful story or book, it's the rewriting. Personally, I hate to rewrite. Many writers feel the same way. All my life I've tried to go forward and not retrace my steps. It's the same with my writing. Once it's written, I want to get on to the next chapter or project. Call it a character defect, if you will.

But I do want the work to be my best. Remember that anything you put out into the world will be the basis for how the world judges you. You want to shine if possible.

How many times should you rewrite? As with everything else in writing, there's isn't one answer that fits everyone. It varies from person to person.

There are people who rewrite tens of times. And there are people like me who keep it to a minimum. I know a guy who makes change after change after change, then goes back and does it all again. I doubt he'll ever submit a "finished" product for publication. It isn't in his nature.

Are you an obsessive type of person? If so, your rewriting may never end. You'll have to find what out what you need to do to satisfy yourself. You'll do this by experimenting, and your process will undoubtedly evolve as you gain more experience over the years.

How do you rewrite? I have to cite the Red King in Lewis Carroll's *Alice in Wonderland*. He had some good advice on the subject: "Begin at the beginning, and go on till you come to the end: then stop."

But you have to know when to call it quits and get on with your life. Be reasonable with yourself. Sometimes "good enough" is good enough. Get on to the next writing project. It's bound to be better.

Vocalizing - A Simple Technique That Works

    Sometimes as I write the first draft, but definitely as I'm working my way through subsequent drafts, I read my text aloud. I rely on my ear for the truth of my sentence structure and checking the sense of what I've written. If I don't get it, my readers won't either.
    When you've finished a section, go through it again on the computer looking for factual gaffes, grammar and spelling errors, and other obvious issues.
    But then go through it again, reading it out loud. This may not be the best advice for deaf writers, but for people with "normal" hearing, it works wonderfully.
    Your ear will tell you the brutal truth; it will not lie to you. Read the section, or even the entire

book, out loud. I'm not talking here about public readings. Read it aloud to yourself, in private. Play all the parts, speak all the dialogue. You'll hear the roughness or smoothness of your work. You'll hear the places it jangles, where it irritates, where it sings.

Fix all the problems, then read it aloud again. You'll be amazed at how this simple technique will improve your writing.

This is not merely an analytical tool or an academic exercise. It's when I have the most fun with my stories. I get to play all the parts, hear each of the characters speak in their own distinctive dialect and accent, and with all the emotive expression they would show if it were real life, or even a movie.

Let's face it; I'm a show off, even when I'm home alone. Vocalizing is great practice for when readying a selection to present to an audience. I've been told I'm an entertaining reader. This practice may be why.

It's great when you're writing, but it's even more helpful when you're editing.

Second (third, fourth, fifth, etc.) time around

Critique Groups

Critique groups can be found in most regions of the country, and there are online crit groups as well. Some are more effective than others, but there is something to be learned by participation in any such group.

I have been running a mystery writers critique group (WNCMysterians.org) in Asheville, North Carolina for several years, and it's been very helpful for all our members. I discovered the model our group follows when I was in a similarly tasked Sisters in Crime critique group near Atlanta. That earlier group took me through my first *Ben Bones* adventure.

The problem with critique groups is finding one that suits you. When I arrived in Asheville, I went to a variety of writers' groups. I didn't bother with groups focused specifically on poetry. That wasn't what I was after. Nor were the memoir groups, or the so-called "literary" groups.

What I discovered was that, although there was a plethora of groups, the typical group was trying to attract writers of all stripes. I'd go to a group and have to sit through several hours of poetry readings, memoir segments, historical pieces, humor, etc., all read by the authors themselves. None of these groups focused on mystery and suspense, and none of them had a clue what a red herring was.

The worst part of one of the groups was that the discussion was not about the writing samples at all. The group members, as a group, attacked the writers. No good. A group has to be supportive of its members and look at the work, not the personal proclivities of its members. So I went out and started my own group, WNCMysterians.org.

I ran an ad in the local newspaper, rented a room at the local library every two weeks, and waited, and waited, and waited. I did this for several months. After a while, someone showed up, a woman who is still a Mysterian six years later. Others showed up and eventually there was a working critique group that knew what a red herring was and when to drop another body through the skylight. These are my type of people.

The WNCMysterians critique for story (plot, internal consistency, etc.). Several members take a broad view of the work. Several of us are more focused on the details of grammar and punctuation. It's a good mix of talents and sensitivities. The group has produced at least ten books by now, all carefully edited by the members. Everyone's writing has improved and we are now a cohesive group of writing friends.

Professional Editors

Editors have to earn a living, too. I've met several professionals. I've heard stories about excellent editors who really know what they're doing, and I've heard some horror stories about expensive charlatans as well.

I have not used a professional fiction or mystery editor myself. Once when I wrote a how-to photography book, the editor assigned by the publisher confronted me on many items that proved she knew nothing about photography. That's a danger, too. If you're going to take your work to a professional editor, be sure the person has experience with your genre.

You also want to get the names and contact information of several of your prospective editor's clients. Call them and listen to what they have to say about the quality of the editorial service and its timeliness. It never hurts to get recommendations.

The Axe as a Writing Tool

In earlier pages I gave some advice about not padding the word count. The goal is not to have 50,000 words, but to have a lean book that says exactly what you mean to say. Fewer and more precise words do a better job than massive paid-by-the-word (or worse, by the pound) verbiage.

In your editing process, cut where possible. Distill your content to its essentials.

Technical Issues

Grammar & Spelling

I had a friend who wrote a book on wild foods. I read it through, decided it was packed with useful information, and undertook to edit it for her. When I was done, I had two large black trash bags full of commas and semicolons that she'd unnecessarily sprinkled liberally throughout. She knew her factual material thoroughly, but she needed a good editor to turn her Johnny Appleseed approach to punctuation into Standard English.

Contrary to the thinking of many a school child, grammar and punctuation are not torture. They are tools for clear understanding. Sure, they can be complex at times, and different editors and publishers may apply their own particular rules to your work, but grammar and punctuation can be learned and manipulated to your advantage.

As the clearest illustration I can think of, allow me to cite the title of that wonderful little book *Eats, Shoots and Leaves* by Lynne Truss. Boy, did she ever get it right! If I only had three books on my shelf, that would be one of them. The other two would be E.B. White's *Elements of Style* and *Roget's Thesaurus*.

Vocabulary & Word Choice

I've used this Mark Twain quote in this book before: "The difference between the right word and the almost right word is the difference between the lightning and the lightning bug." This is such an important thought that I've even put it on one of my business cards.

Memorize this quote. Apply it daily in your life. Quote it to friends and enemies alike. Be a bore at parties.

Put a copy of *Roget's Thesaurus* in the bathroom for casual perusal. Your vocabulary will improve and you'll always be able to say exactly what you mean.

Publishing

A Changed World

It used to be that people would go to a book store, browse a bit, then buy a book or two. No longer. Now they go online to buy and they read electronic versions.

The Traditional route

Writers used to be able to approach publishers directly. We could mail in unsolicited manuscripts and they might be read. These were informal submissions and were described as coming in "over the transom." Then things became more complicated. If you didn't have an agent, you couldn't get your work in front of a publisher. They'd closed and locked the transom.

That was all right for the old guard of established authors. They already had agents, reputations, and "real" publishers, complete with publicity agents and marketing departments. But how was a struggling new writer supposed to get an agent?

That was easy. When you had a book contract offer from a publisher, you'd bring it to the agent of your choice and he/she would negotiate the best deal for you. Otherwise, an agent wouldn't talk to you. They were too busy with their paying clients.

Wait a minute. That sounds like a conundrum, a *Catch-22*. You couldn't get your work to a publisher without an agent, and you couldn't get an agent without a publisher's offer. Yikes!

Personally, I've been through the futile exercise of approaching agents many times, all to no avail. It's been several years since I tried, but the world has changed.

Self-publishing

Fed up with the traditional route? How much courage can you muster? As W.C. Fields said, "There comes a time in the affairs of man when he must take the bull by the tail and face the situation." That's exactly what I did.

I had been my own publisher with the two national magazines I put out in the 1990s. Being a lousy businessman, I used my own money.

Eventually, I went broke. Do I regret the experience? Sure, I regret losing the money, but I'm pleased about accomplishing something I'd always wanted to do.

But then the Internet appeared and it became possible to publish electronically: blogs, magazines, even entire books. With trepidation, I dove into the electronic sea, swam out to deep water, and began publishing my writings.

The Electronic World

We have entered a new era. It's now possible to publish without an agent or a publisher, but it takes determination and courage. Do you have the geek potential to do it yourself?

(Author's note: "geek" is not an insult. It is a term of respect. A geek is a person who knows more than other people, in however limited a subject area.)

Not being personally "computer savvy" is no excuse. If you can organize and write a competent book, you can also find someone to do the final formatting for you.

You can publish a strictly electronic version, or through what are known as BOD (books-on-demand) businesses, you can have physical books printed and shipped to your customers one at a time without having to invest thousands of dollars in an inventory that will fill your garage or basement and be passed on to your ungrateful and complaining heirs. Amazon's CreateSpace (https://www.createspace.com) and Ingram's Lightning Source (https://www1.lightningsource.com/) are two of the reputable biggies. Do some research on your own and comparison shopping. Contact some of the authors and listen to their experiences before you commit. There are opportunistic charlatans out there in the electronic world as well as legitimate businesses.

Selling books

The problem of selling written work is now on the shoulders of the individual author. Whether fact or fiction, history or memoir, poetry or how-to, it's up to us now.

Look around you next time you're in a medico's waiting room, at the airport, or in any restaurant. A notable percentage of the people will be reading electronic books on their tablet computers. These people are your market.

Fiction is a particularly tough sell. Part of your problem is that everyone who thinks they have a book in them is sitting down to write, and because publishing is free, there's an immense amount of inferior material available nowadays for your deathless work to get buried in. Even if they're competently written, many works are never edited and are full of typos and grammatical errors. As Ambrose Bierce once said of another author's work, "The covers of this book are too far apart." Too true, too true.

But even in the face of all that, good writing is good writing, and cynic though I am, I'm optimistic enough to think that a good book will eventually find its audience. In fact, I'm banking on it.

Appendices

Recommended Reading – Mystery Authors

    This author list is by no means a complete list of greats. It's the leanest, most basic listing, a few folks I've found enjoyable myself, and who've set good examples for me as a reader and writer. Read voraciously in your genre. You'll find many other authors who suit your tastes. Remember, this entire endeavor, both reading and writing, is all as subjective as can be. What suits one will be anathema to another. Find your own path.

    Lawrence Block - Besides being the author of dozens of entertaining books, Mr. Block has written on the subject of writing professionally, *Telling Lies for Fun and Profit*. He's documented his methods and given advice to upcoming authors in the pages of *Writer's Digest* for years. Those opinions (opinions, not rules) have been compiled into several volumes that are rich in unique viewpoint and quality advice. Just because a book was released years ago doesn't negate its inner truths.

Raymond Chandler - You might not know it, but Chandler wrote *Double Indemnity* and *The Big Sleep*, two of the great mystery films.

Arthur Conan Doyle - Dare I try to convince you to read some Sherlock Holmes tales? That's like carrying coals to Newcastle, if you catch my drift. By the way, if you don't know what that means, you'd better learn some of those old sayings that have become today's lichens. They actually mean something. They may even have the nugget in them that becomes the focal point of your next story because of their inner sense.

Janet Evonovich - Yes, she's entertaining. I love the insanity of her scenes. And I loved her characters when first I met them. Everyone does. The first of her Stephanie Plum books was great, and so were several that followed, but after a while they became boring. Same story, same characters, same lovers, same dilemmas: same, same, same. I can't argue with her success, but don't do it that way.

If you're going to have a series character, with or without series cohorts, vary the situations. Invent new problems for them to solve. Put them in different geographies. Create variety so the characters, and thus the books, aren't predictable.

Sue Grafton - Ah, pure pleasure. Kinsey Millhone is a jewel of a character. Sure, she has personal and family baggage that she carries through her adventures, but it's not overwhelming and it provides depth for her instead of crushing weight. She's relatively sane, logical, and thorough in her investigations. In short, she's a proper sleuth. Most important, her cases are of differing sorts, featuring a variety of problems and goals. Frankly, she was a prime exemplar when I was developing my own serial character, Ben Bones.

Dashiell Hammett - It's been noted that Dash Hammett was a "cinematic" author. What does this mean? It means he followed that old writers' maxim to show, not to tell. If you watch the Humphrey Bogart film *The Maltese Falcon* with the remote in one hand and the book in the other, you'll see how the film tracks the book line for line. Hammett showed everything necessary, eschewed the irrelevant, and his stories were stronger for it. His tales were spare and clean. Study this. Learn this approach.

Michael Havelin - Read my Ben Bones series for examples of good and bad writing, tricky and linear plots, red herrings, and other related sense and nonsense. I learned a great deal writing them. Maybe there's something for you to learn from them, too.

Stephen King - I don't particularly care to read his voluminous horror tales, but I have read and reread his advice to writers, *On Writing*. Get hold of it, read it, study it, and go back to it once in a while. The guy knows what he's talking about.

Walter Mosely – For setting, sense of place, and characters, Mosely can't be beaten. Study this man's work.

Sara Paretsky - Paretsky's V.I. Warshawski is, to my mind, one of the great private detectives. Her background, her adventures, her inner life, all ring clearly to me. I go back to her again and again. Of course, the fact that she's been portrayed rather wonderfully on film by Kathleen Turner doesn't hurt either.

Robert B. Parker - Spenser is another series character who continues to inspire. Sometimes the character involvements get a bit stale for me, but the mystery and adventure side of the stories are always varied and intriguing.

Recommended Reading – Reference

Larry Beinhart, *How to Write a Mystery*, Ballantine Books, New York, 1996. ISBN 0-345-39758-4.

André Bernard, *Now All We Need is a Title – Famous Book Titles and How They Got that Way*, W.W. Norton, New York, 1951. ISBN 0-393-31436-7. Entertaining reading that will make you think twice, perhaps thrice, about your title.

Lawrence Block, *Telling Lies for Fun & Profit – A Manual for Fiction Writers*, Quill – William Morrow, 1981. ISBN 0-688-13228-6. A compilation of entertaining and insightful columns on writing from the pages of *Writer's Digest*.

Lawrence Block, *Writing the Novel – From Plot to Print*, Writers Digest Books, 1979, ISBN 0-89879-208-8.

John A. Carr, *The Craft of Crime – Conversations With Crime Writers*, Houghton Mifflin Company, Boston, 1983. ISBN 0-395-33121-8. A collection of revealing conversations with some top mystery writers.

Hallie Ephron, *Writing and Selling Your Mystery Novel*, Writer's Digest Books, 2005. ISBN 1-58297-317-2. Contains plenty of interactive exercises.

Farrell and Tish, *Write Your Own Mystery Story*, Compass Point Books, 2006. ISBN 978-0756518165.

James N. Frey, *How to Write a Damn Good Mystery*, St. Martin's Press, 2004. ISBN 978-0312304461.

Sue Grafton, Ed., *Writing Mysteries*, A Handbook, 2nd ed. Mystery Writers of America, 2002. ISBN 978-0898795028.

G. Miki Hayden, *Writing the Mystery*,

Intrigue Press, 2004. ISBN 978-1890768638.

Patricia Highsmith, *Plotting and Writing Suspense Fiction*, St. Martin's Griffin, 2001. ISBN 978-0312286668.

P.D. James, *Talking About Detective Fiction*, Knopf, 2009, ISBN 978-0307592828

Isobel Lambot, *How to Write Crime Novels*, Virgin Publishing, London, 1992, ISBN 0-74900-125-9. A view from the other side of the pond.

Margaret Lucke, *Writing Mysteries*, Self-Counsel Press, 1999. ISBN 978-1551802053.

Barbara Norville, *Writing the Modern Mystery*, Writers Digest Books, 1992.ISBN 978-0898795233.

Shannon O'Cork, *How to Write Mysteries*, Writers Digest Books, 1989. ISBN 978-0898793727.

Robert J. Randisi, *Writing the Private Eye Novel*, Writers Digest Books, 1997. ISBN 978-0898797671.

Gillian Roberts, *You Can Write a Mystery*, Writers Digest Books, 1999. ISBN 978-0898798630.

Chris Roerden, *Don't Murder Your Mystery*, Bella Rosa Books, Rock Hill, SC, 2006. ISBN 1-933523-13-1. Great advice from a long-time professional editor.

John Paxton Sheriff, *Writing Crime Novels*, Robert Hale, 2001, ISBN 978-0709068365.

William Strunk, Jr. & E.B. White, *The Elements of Style*, The Macmillan Company. This book never goes out of style. It will steer you right when it comes to basic American English grammar and usage.

William G. Tapply, *The Elements of Mystery Fiction: Writing the Modern Whodunit*, 2 ed., Poisoned Pen Press, 2004. ISBN 978-1590581155.

Lynne Truss, *Eats, Shoots & Leaves*, Gotham Books, 2003. ISBN 978-1-592-40391-2. Foibles of English punctuation. Doomed to become a classic.

Useful Websites

Dictionary	http://dictionary.reference.com/
National Novel Writing Month (NaNoWriMo). Write a 50010 word novel during the 30 days of November. That's only 1667 words per day. You can do it if you try.	http://www.nanowrimo.org/
Sisters in Crime	http://sistersincrime.org/
Thesaurus	http://thesaurus.com/
WNC Mysterians Critique Group	http://wncmysterians.org/
yWriter software	http://www.spacejock.com/yWriter5.html

Critique Group Procedures

What follows are procedures adapted from methods I learned as a novice member of a critique group that was a subgroup of the Atlanta Sisters in Crime chapter. The crit group helped me through the morass of my first Ben Bones adventure. I took what worked, added a few things, deleted others, and have successfully used this plan for WNCMysterians.org. Believe me, it works. Take what works for you, adapt it all to the dynamics of your group, be supportive of one another, and be productive.

WNCMysterians Critique Group Procedures

Group will meet every two weeks. Maximum group size is eight (8). Schedule changes and other decisions will be by majority agreement. Donations from participants will help defray expenses (ex: room rental fee, copying, etc.)

Prospective members must submit a writing sample and synopsis of their current project. Group will evaluate and vote on acceptance or rejection.

Participants can submit up to 10-15 pages at a time to all regular members for critique. The goal here is to give more people more crit time. Submissions will be made via email. If needed for readability by everyone, group leader will convert submission to pdf and forward to members.

Discussion will be on the basis of the prepared critiques, not on live readings.

Critiques by participants may be made on story printouts or separate sheet referenced to the submission and submitted to the author at the next crit session or beforehand via email.

Critiques will emphasize constructive criticism, not author bashing. Be polite, but be honest. We're there to support one another and move the work forward.

Critiques will cite specific problems, i.e. where the reader lost interest, irritating character traits, discontinuities in behavior or site, plot issues, factual errors in technical matters, etc.

Author should not respond to crit the first time around the group. After the first round, author can respond or seek clarification.

If author's material is read aloud at crit sessions, it must be read by a neutral party, not by the author.

Consider grammar, spelling & punctuation to be "second tier" concerns. Although important, these are mechanical issues and need to be mentioned, but not dwelt on.

At various times, the group might decide to research and discuss various topics of interest to authors. The following is a list of possible discussion topics. Add more of your own.

- finding ideas
- research & factual errors
- writing style
- vocabulary
- situation
- setting – time/place/weather, etc.
- plot & structure
- character development
- dialogue
- exposition
- description/mood/atmosphere
- foreshadowing (weaving in clues)
- clues (real and red herrings)
- using all 5 senses
- editing/self editing (macro & micro)
- writing habits
- handling large projects (planning, outlining,

notes en route, word count)
- rewriting
- agents
- publishers
- marketing
- anything else pertinent to writing and/or getting published.

Index

ADHD, 140
Alcohol, 65, 72
Agents, 163
Alice in Wonderland, 143
Alien, 88
Amateur Crime Solver, 42
Amazon.com, 154
Antagonists, 88
Appleseed, Johnny, 150
Arson, 60
Asheville, 5, 146
Assassin's Dilemma, The, 25
Assault, 52
Bacall, Lauren, 132
Batman, 88
Battery, 52
Ben Bones and the Conventional Murders, 133
Bierce, Ambrose, 155
Big Sleep, The, 132, 157
Black's Law Dictionary, 36, 44
Blackmail, 57
Block, Lawrence, 17, 156
Books-on-demand, 154
BOD, 154
Bogart, Humphrey, 132, 158
Bones, Ben, 42, 95, 117, 122, 125, 133, 157
Breaking and entering, 56
Bronson, Charles, 59
Brown, Birmingham, 95
Bruce, Nigel, 95
Bully
Burglary, 56
Burroughs, Edgar Rice, 24
Cardinal Richelieu, 99
Carter, John, 24
Carroll, Lewis, 143

Catch-22, 152
Cause of Death, 75
Chan, Charlie, 95
Chandler, Raymond, 34, 92, 115, 132, 157
Chapter, 126
Characters, 84, 163
Character description, 89
Characters, Minor, 105
Characters, sources of, 87
Christie, Agatha, 24, 33
Citizens' Police Academy, 38, 39, 104
CIS, 37
Cliff hanger, 120
Clues & Anti-clues See also Red Herring), 137, 163
Coleridge, Samuel Taylor, 29
Comic relief, 96
Connolly, Michael, 24, 35
Continuity, 121
Conversion, 55
Cops, 103
Cozy, 33
Count de Rochefort, 99
CreateSpace, 154, 162
Critique groups, 146
Crumb, R., 118
Darwin Awards, 81
Death Wish, 59
Description, 163
deus ex machine, 137
Dialogue, 130, 133, 163
Dick, Phillip K., 91
Dickens, Charles, 124
dictionary.com, 140
Do Androids Dream of Electric Sheep, 91
Dollar, Johnny, 107
Double Indemnity, 157
Doyle, Arthur Conan, 24, 40, 157
Doyle, Popeye, 37
Dragnet
Drugs, 58, 65, 73

Dumas, Alexander, 99
Eats, Shoots and Leaves, 150
Editors & Editing, 148, 163
Electronic World, 154
Elements of Style, 150
Euterpe, 12
Evonovich, Janet, 92, 157
Exercises, 27, 36, 39, 41, 43, 49, 53, 57, 77, 91, 93, 96, 98, 100, 102, 104, 109, 115, 119, 134, 136
Extortion, 57
Extra Body, The, 113
Fields, W.C., 153
Flashback, 125
Flash-forward, 125
Floor plan, 133
Foreshadowing, 120, 163
Fraud, 55-56
French Connection, The, 37
Fu Manchu, 88
Gandalf, 88
Geek, 154
Genres, 32
God mode (Omniscient narrator) (See Point of View)
Google, 26, 27, 123
Grafton, Sue, 24, 157
Grammar, 150
Greed, 66-67
Grisham, John
Grafton, Sue, 40, 92, 107
Gunn, Peter, 34
Hammer, Mike, 34
Hammett, Dashiell, 34, 115, 158
Hate crime, 72
Hatfields & McCoys, 70
Havelin, Michael, 158, 173
Heinlein, Robert, 30
Hemingway, Ernest, 80
Henchman (henchmen), 99
Hero (See Protagonist)
Hero's Journey, 123, 124

Hill Street Blues, 37
Holmes, Sherlock, 24, 40, 88, 95, 108, 140, 157
Homicide, 47
Hook, 118
Human trafficking, 54
Ideas, sources of, 81, 163
Immigration, Illegal, 54
Intent, 65
Internet, 24, 28, 133
Jealousy, 71
Joker, The, 88
Juvenal, 70
Kersey, Paul, 59
Key Largo, 132
Kidnapping, 19, 54
King, Stephen, 158
Kubla Khan, 29
Kurosawa, 126
Larceny, 44
Law, Jude, 95
Legal Thriller, 35
Les Misérables, 67
Leiningen Versus the Ants, 88
Lightning Source, 154
Lincoln, Abraham, 22
Lincoln Lawyer, 24, 35
Linear mode, 125
Lola, 95
Lord of the Rings, 88
Love, 71
Love interest, 101-102
Luthor, Lex, 88
Manner of Death, 74
Maltese Falcon, The, 158
Manslaughter, 49
Marketing, 154, 163
Marlowe, Phillip, 34, 92, 95, 132
Marple, Miss, 24, 33, 42
Mason, Perry, 35
Maugham, W. Somerset, 15

McBain, Ed, 37
Mechanism of Death, 75
Milhone, Kinsey, 24, 40, 92, 95, 107, 157
Misdemeanor larceny, 44
Momentum, 127
Money laundering, 61
Morelli, Joe, 95
Moriarty, Professor, 88
Mosely, Walter, 158
Motive, 21, 65
Mr. Natural, 118
Murder (see Homicide), 19, 47, 49
Muse, 12, 30
Mystery Mastery, 4
NaNoWriMo, 113, 114, 117, 161
Narrative arc, 123
National Novel Writing Month (See NaNoWriMo)
NCIS, 37
New York Times, 4
News of the Weird, 81
Noir, 34
North Carolina, 48, 52, 56, 60, 63
North Carolina Crimes, 36
North Carolina General Statutes, 44
Omniscient narrator (God mode) (See Point of View)
On Writing, 158
Opening Situation, 117
Outline, 112, 114, 163
Pacing, 128-129
Pascal, Blaise, 80
Paretsky, Sara, 24, 158
Parker, Robert B., 40, 115, 158
Pedophilia, 19, 63
Penguin, The, 88
Perfect Storm, The, 88
Person, First (See Point of View)
Person, Second (See Point of View)
Person, Third (See Point of View)
PI, 40
Pimp, 63

Place, 28
Plot, 110, 116, 163
Plum, Stephanie, 92, 95, 157
Point of View (POV), 106-108
Poirot, Hercule, 33
Police Procedural, 37
POV (See Point of View)
Power, 68
Private investigator, 40
Profit motive (See Greed)
Prologue, 117-118
Protagonist, 92
Prostitution, 62
Publishers & Publishing, 152, 163
Punctuation, 163
Ranger, 95
Rape, 52
Rathbone, Basil, 140
Reading aloud
Red herring (See Clues), 139, 163
Red King, 143
Research, 24, 132, 163
Revenge, 70
Reverse Mode, 126
Ride Along Program, 38, 104
Ripley, 88
Robbery, 50
Robinson, Edward G., 132
Rochester, New York, 25
Roshamon, 126
Rules, 15, 30-31
San Francisco, 34
Sauron, 88
Scene, 127
Scrivener, 127
Self-discipline, 30-31, 140
Self-publishing, 153
Senses, 135, 163
Sensory environment, 135
Serpico, 37

Setting, 131, 163
Sex & sex crimes, 19, 62
Shakespeare, William, 112
Sidekicks, 95
Sisters in Crime, 146, 161
Six Degrees of Kevin Bacon, 25
Six degrees of separation, 23, 104
Skywalker, Luke, 88
Slavery, 19, 54
Smith, Denis Nayland, 88
Smith & Wesson, 121
Spade, Sam, 34
Spelling, 150
Spenser, 34, 40, 115, 158
Spy Kids 2: The Island of Lost Dreams, 116
Standard English, 150
Star Wars, 88
Stephenson, Carl, 88
Stephenson, Robert Lewis, 124
Sternwood, Carmen, 132
Sternwood, General, 132
Story arc, 123
Suicide, 75
Superman, 88
Tarzan, 24
Telling Lies for Fun and Profit, 156
Terrorism, 19
Theft (See Conversion)
Theft by trick, 55
Thesaurus, Roget's, 29, 79, 150, 151
thesaurus.com, 140, 161
Three Musketeers, The, 99
Truss, Lynn, 150
Twain, Mark, 79, 150
Vader, Darth, 88
Valjean, Jean, 67
Villain, 97, 116
Vocabulary, 150, 163
Vocalizing, 144
Warshawski, V.I., 24, 95, 158

Watson, Dr., 24, 88, 95, 108
Weapons, 76-78
Weaver, Sigourney, 88
White, E.B., 150
Wikipedia, 25
Writer's Digest, 156
WNCMysterians.org, 5, 146, 147, 161, 162
Writer's block, 13
Yours Truly, Johnny Dollar
yWriter, 127, 161

About the Author

Michael Havelin was born and raised in Yonkers, New York. He attended college at the Rochester Institute of Technology, earning degrees in Photography and Filmmaking, then went on to graduate from the University of Florida Holland Law Center.

Michael has worked as a musician (rock, swing, blues), author (articles, how-to photo books & mysteries, including the Ben Bones series of genealogical mysteries), filmmaker (writer/director of commercials and documentaries), photographer (environmental journalism & motorcycle road-racing), teacher (computers, photography, writing), lawyer (uncivil practice), editor, publisher (two national magazines and several books), web designer, woodworker, and interpreter (English/American Sign Language). He has been a guest presenter at Killer Nashville (2012) and Blue Ridge Bookfest (2014). Since 2009, he has run WNCMysterians.org, a mystery writers' critique group in Asheville, NC.

Yankee by birth, Michael now lives and creates in Asheville, North Carolina.

michaelhavelin.com
WNCMysterians.org

benbones.com

Look for Michael Havelin's other books online, in book stores and libraries.

Ben Bones and the Deadly Descendants

Ben Bones and the Search for Paneta's Crown

Ben Bones and the Galleon of Gold

The Extra Body

Palaver's Hands

The Embezzler Didn't

Bloody-Minded Fictions

The Cat Eater

www.ingramcontent.com/pod-product-compliance
Lightning Source LLC
Chambersburg PA
CBHW060534100426
42743CB00009B/1524